Q. HORATI FLACCI

CARMINUM LIBER I

Q. HORATI FLACCI
CARMINUM LIBER I

WITH INTRODUCTION AND NOTES

BY

JAMES GOW

CAMBRIDGE:
AT THE UNIVERSITY PRESS
1949

CAMBRIDGE UNIVERSITY PRESS
Cambridge, New York, Melbourne, Madrid, Cape Town,
Singapore, São Paulo, Delhi, Mexico City

Cambridge University Press
The Edinburgh Building, Cambridge CB2 8RU, UK

Published in the United States of America by Cambridge University Press, New York

www.cambridge.org
Information on this title: www.cambridge.org/9781107667020

© Cambridge University Press 1895

First published 1895
First Edition 1895
Reprinted 1904, 1917, 1923, 1934, 1944, 1949
First paperback edition 2013

A catalogue record for this publication is available from the British Library

ISBN 978-1-107-66702-0 Paperback

PREFACE.

THIS edition of Horace's Odes and Epodes was under-
taken at the request of the Syndics of the Pitt Press.

In the text, at a few notorious passages, I have admitted
conjectures which give a good sense with very little alteration of the letters. The spelling is, for obvious reasons,
adapted in the main to that of Lewis and Short's lexicon.
In regard to final *-es* and *-is* in acc. plur. of the 3rd declen-
sion I have almost always followed the indications given in
Keller's *Epilegomena*.

In preparing the notes, I have used Orelli's edition (as
revised in 1885 by Hirschfelder) freely for illustrative quo-
tations. It is the common quarry. Besides this, I have
referred very often to the editions of A. Kiessling (1884)
and Dean Wickham (1874), less frequently to those of
Mr Page (1886), C. W. Nauck (1880) and H. Schütz (1874).
The dates given are the dates of my copies.

I am greatly indebted to my friend Dr Postgate, of
Trinity College, for many corrections and suggestions.

J. G.

NOTTINGHAM,
October, 1895.

CONTENTS.

INTRODUCTION.

§ 1.   *Life of Horace.*

OUR knowledge of the life of Horace is derived chiefly from
his own works, which teem with allusions to his past history
and present occupations. A few minor details are supplied
either by the scholiasts or by a brief biography of the poet
which is found in some MSS. and which may be attributed
with certainty to Suetonius (C. Suetonius Tranquillus, flor.
A.D. 150).

Quintus Horatius Flaccus[1] was born on the 8th of December[2]
B.C. 65[3] at Venusia, an ancient military colony situated near
Mt. Voltur and the river Aufidus, on the confines of Apulia and
Lucania[4].

Horace's father was a freedman, possibly a Greek by birth[5].

---

[1] For the full name cf. *Sat.* II. 6. 37, *Carm.* IV. 6. 44, *Epod.* 15. 12.

[2] For the month cf. *Epist.* I. 20. 27.   The day is supplied by
Suetonius.

[3] Horace names the year by the consul L. Manlius Torquatus, *Carm.*
III. 21. 1 (*nata mecum consule Manlio*) and *Epod.* 13. 6.

[4] For Mt. Voltur, see *Carm.* III. 4. 10.   For the rest, *Carm.* IV. 9. 2
(*longe sonantem natus ad Aufidum*), *Sat.* II. 1. 34, 35 (*Lucanus an
Appulus anceps | nam Venusinus arat finem sub utrumque colonus*), and
Sat. I. 6. 73 (where the Venusian boys are said to be *magnis e
centurionibus orti*).

[5] *Sat.* I. 6. 6 (*me libertino patre natum*).   The foundation for the
suggestion that the father was a Greek is merely (1) that he had been a

By profession, he was a tax-collector or debt-collector[1], perhaps also a dealer in salt-fish (*salsamentarius*), if Suetonius may be trusted. From small beginnings[2], he seems to have acquired some fortune, sufficient, at any rate, to warrant him in removing from Venusia to Rome, and devoting himself to his son's education[3]. To his father's fond and judicious care of him, during his school days, Horace more than once bears eloquent testimony[4].

At Rome, Horace was put to an expensive school[5], kept by a crusty old grammarian, L. Orbilius Pupillus, nicknamed 'the flogger.' Here he studied, among other things, the early Latin poets[6] (such as Livius Andronicus) and the *Iliad* of Homer[7].

From school Horace proceeded (about the age of 19, no doubt) to the university of Athens, where he attended the lectures of the Academy[8]. The course would include geometry, logic, moral philosophy and probably also rhetoric or literary criticism. In after years, Horace no longer adhered to the

slave and must have been a foreigner, and (2) that Horace at an early age was sufficiently fluent in Greek to write Greek verses (*Sat.* I. 10. 31—35). It is not known how the father acquired the name of Horatius. According to usage, Flaccus ('flap-eared') would have been his slave-name and Horatius the name of his former master. (See Dict. of Antiq. 3rd ed. s. v. *Nomen.*) The colony of Venusia was enrolled in the *tribus Horatia*, and the father may have been a slave in the service of the town.

[1] *Sat.* I. 6. 86 (*ut fuit ipse, coactor*).

[2] *Sat.* I. 6. 71 (*macro pauper agello*).

[3] *Sat.* I. 6. 71—96, esp. 81, 82 (*ipse mihi custos incorruptissimus omnes | circum doctores aderat*).

[4] Besides *Sat.* I. 6, see also *Sat.* I. 4. 105 sqq.

[5] *Sat.* I. 6. 76—80.

[6] *Epist.* II. 1. 69—71 (*non equidem insector delendave carmina Livi | esse reor, memini quae plagosum mihi parvo | Orbilium dictare*).

[7] *Epist.* II. 2. 41, 42 (*Romae nutriri mihi contigit atque doceri | iratus Grais quantum nocuisset Achilles*).

[8] *Epist.* II. 2. 44, 45 (*adiecere bonae paullo plus artis Athenae, | scilicet ut vellem curvo dinoscere rectum | atque inter silvas Academi quaerere verum*).

Academic opinions in moral philosophy, but professed himself a free thinker inclined to Epicureanism[1].

During his stay at Athens, Horace made the acquaintance of many young Romans of noble birth[2], by whom apparently he was introduced, in September B.C. 44, to M. Junius Brutus[3], the Liberator. Brutus, at this time, was passing through Athens on his way to the province of Macedonia which had been assigned to him (as propraetor) by Julius Caesar before his murder. (Cassius meanwhile was proceeding to his province, Syria.) As governor of Macedonia, Brutus was collecting an army, partly to oppose C. Antonius, who claimed the province as nominee of the senate, and partly to combat some turbulent tribes of Thracians, who were harassing the borders. In this army, Horace received the appointment of military tribune[4]. He marched with the troops through Macedonia and Thrace, crossed the Hellespont, saw a good deal of Asia Minor[5] and returned with the combined forces of Brutus and Cassius to the field of Philippi (Nov. B.C. 42). In the first battle at this place, Brutus was victorious ; in the second (twenty days later) he was defeated, and Horace fled[6], never to bear arms again.

---

[1] *Epist.* I. 1. 14 (*nullius addictus iurare in verba magistri*), and *Epist.* I. 4. 16 (*Epicuri de grege porcum*). Cf. also *Carm.* I. 34. 1—5.

[2] Some of them are named in *Sat.* I. 10. 81—87.

[3] Plutarch, *Brutus*, 24.

[4] *Sat.* I. 6. 48 (*quod mihi pareret legio Romana tribuno*). The statement here is doubtless an exaggeration, for there should have been six tribunes to the legion.

[5] It is clear that Horace was at Clazomenae and saw the trial described in *Sat.* I. 7. The rest of his campaigning, before Philippi, is mere matter of inference. He speaks of Thrace in winter (e.g. *Carm.* I. 37. 20) and of the Hellespont (*Epist.* I. 3. 4) as if he had seen them, and he addresses a friend (*Carm.* II. 7. 1, 2) as ' *O saepe mecum tempus in ultimum | deducte Bruto militiae duce.*'

[6] *Carm.* II. 7. 9, 10 (*tecum Philippos et celerem fugam | sensi, relicta non bene parmula*). Cf. also *Carm.* III. 4. 26. In *Epod.* I. 16 (written ten years later than Philippi) he describes himself as *imbellis ac firmus parum.*

Soon after the battle, Horace appears to have obtained a pardon from Octavianus and leave to return to Rome. He seems to have travelled nearly all the way by sea and suffered shipwreck, or came near it, at Mons Palinurus on the Lucanian coast[1]. His father was by this time dead, and when he reached Rome, he found himself penniless[2]. It is said that he managed to procure a situation as clerk in some department of the public treasury[3] and that he held this office for about four years (B.C. 41—37). Horace himself says that poverty drove him to making verses[2], but it is unlikely that he found poetry a source of income. More probably he had introductions to some conservative (i.e. republican) coteries, and used his literary talents to make himself welcome, in spite of his poverty. No other society would have received with favour, at that time, such denunciations of civil war as Epodes 7 and 16, two of Horace's earliest pieces.

The compositions of Horace at this period were undoubtedly either satires in the manner of Lucilius (died B.C. 103), or iambic epodes, mostly satirical, in the manner of Archilochus of Paros[4] (flor. B.C. 700). Through these, probably, he obtained the acquaintance of L. Varius and Vergil, who became his fast friends and introduced him to Maecenas[5]. Some nine months

---

[1] *Carm.* III. 4. 28 and 27. 18.

[2] *Epist.* II. 2. 49—52. (*unde simul primum me dimisere Philippi,* | *decisis humilem pennis inopemque paterni* | *et laris et fundi paupertas impulit audax* | *ut versus facerem.*)

[3] The authorities are Suetonius, who says *scriptum quaestorium comparavit,* and the scholiasts to *Sat.* II. 6. 36.

[4] *Epist.* I. 19. 23—25 (*Parios ego primus iambos* | *ostendi Latio*). The oldest of the published works is *Sat.* I. 7, which seems to have been written in B.C. 43 or early in 42. *Epode* 16 seems to have been written on hearing the news of the capture of Perusia, B.C. 40. *Sat.* I. 2 and 4 were written before Horace became intimate with Maecenas. *Epode* 7 is assigned to B.C. 36.

[5] *Sat.* I. 6. 54, 55 (*optimus olim* | *Vergilius, post hunc Varius dixere quid essem*).

afterwards (B.C. 38)[1] Maecenas invited him to join his circle, and Horace's fortune was made.

C. Cilnius Maecenas was now and for long afterwards the right-hand man of Octavianus in all civil affairs. He was very rich, very fond of literary society, and very generous to literary men. His patronage relieved Horace from poverty and from anxiety about his social position, while it provided the necessary stimulus to a poet who was naturally both lazy and fastidious. The subsequent life of Horace has only a few prominent incidents. In the autumn of B.C. 38 he was one of a large party who accompanied Maecenas to Brundisium[2]. In B.C. 35 he published the first book of the Satires. Soon afterwards Maecenas gratified his dearest wish by presenting him with the small estate in the Sabine district[3], to which so many loving allusions are made in Horace's works. It seems to have been his habit, at least in later years, to spend the summer and autumn here[4], the winter at Baiae or Velia or some other sea-side resort, and only the spring at Rome[5]. It is likely that Horace was present as a spectator at the battle of Actium in B.C. 31[6]. In B.C. 30 he published the second book of the Satires and, about the same time, the Epodes. About B.C. 23 he published the first three books of the Odes together.

It is obvious, in these works, that the political opinions of Horace had undergone a great change since he fought for the republic at Philippi. By B.C. 31 he had learnt to exult in the

---

[1] *Ibidem*, 61, 62 (*revocas nono post mense iubesque | esse in amicorum numero*). The year is fixed by *Sat.* II. 6. 40, 41, where Horace says that it is nearly eight years since *Maecenas me coepit habere suorum | in numero*. This satire was written at the end of B.C. 31.

[2] The journey is described in *Sat.* I. 5.

[3] The fullest description is in *Epist.* I. 16. The estate lay in the valley of the Digentia, north of Tibur.

[4] *Epist.* I. 16. 15, 16. (*hae latebrae dulces, etiam, si credis, amoenae, | incolumem tibi me praestant Septembribus horis.*)

[5] *Epist.* I. 7. 1—12.

[6] *Epod.* 1 and 9.

victory at Actium and to hail Caesar as the saviour of society[1]. But there is no sign, even as late as B.C. 20, when the first book of Epistles was published, that Horace was intimate with the emperor. Augustus was perhaps too busy, and too often absent from Rome[2], to cultivate the poet's acquaintance. But the intimacy, whenever it began[3], was of great importance to Horace. He yielded to Augustus what he had refused to Maecenas[4], and resumed the writing of lyric poetry, which he had meant to abandon. Thus in B.C. 17 he wrote the *Carmen Saeculare* by command, and about B.C. 14 the odes *Carm.* IV. 4 and 14, which formed the nucleus of the fourth book. Suetonius, who tells us this, tells us also that *Epist.* II. 1 was written at the express request of Augustus, who wished his name to be connected with a composition of this class[5].

The Fourth Book of the Odes was published about B.C. 14, the Second Book of the Epistles about B.C. 12[6]. It is observable that in these works the name of Maecenas is no longer prominent. The first Satire of the first book, the first Epode, the first Ode, the first Epistle had all been addressed to him in

---

[1] *Epod.* 9. *Carm.* I. 2 and 37.

[2] He was absent from Rome B.C. 31 to 29 and 27 to 24: was very ill in 23, and was absent again B.C. 22—19 (October).

[3] *Epist.* I. 9 shows that Horace had some acquaintance with Tiberius before B.C. 20, and perhaps *Epist.* I. 13 shows as much acquaintance with Augustus.

[4] *Epist.* I. 1.

[5] Suetonius says, "scripta quidem eius (Augustus) usque adeo probavit mansuraque perpetuo opinatus est, ut non modo saeculare carmen componendum iniunxerit, sed et Vindelicam victoriam Tiberii Drusique privignorum suorum, eumque coegerit propter hoc tribus carminum libris ex longo intervallo quartum addere: post sermones vero quosdam lectos nullam sui mentionem habitam ita sit questus 'irasci me tibi scito, quod non in plerisque eiusmodi scriptis mecum potissimum loquaris. An vereris ne apud posteros infame tibi sit, quod videaris familiaris nobis esse?' Expressitque eclogam ad se cuius initium est: '*Cum tot ustineas*,' etc."

[6] The date of the *Ars Poetica* is very uncertain.

grateful homage for his kindness, but there is no allusion to him in the later publications save an affectionate record of his birthday in *Carm.* IV. II. It is known, from Tacitus (*Ann.* III. 30), that after B.C. 20 there was a coolness between Maecenas and Augustus[1]. It is clear, too, from Suetonius, that Augustus made efforts to detach Horace from Maecenas, first by offering him a secretaryship, which was declined, and afterwards by encouraging him to familiarity and giving him handsome presents[2]. One may imagine, therefore, that Horace was in an awkward and unhappy position. He was not easy with Augustus but dared not offend him, and perhaps his compliance with the emperor's commands roused some jealousy in Maecenas. But the estrangement, if there was one, between the poet and his patron did not endure. On his deathbed, Maecenas wrote to Augustus 'Horati Flacci, ut mei, memor esto.' He died early in B.C. 8, and Horace followed him to the grave in the same year, on November 27th.

Horace describes himself, in B.C. 20, as 'short, prematurely grey, fond of the sunshine, quick-tempered but easily appeased[3].' Some account of his daily habits in Rome and in the country

[1] Augustus had an intrigue with Maecenas' wife, Terentia, but Tacitus does not mention this.

[2] The following extracts from Suetonius' life of Horace will suffice: 'Augustus epistularum quoque officium obtulit, ut hoc ad Maecenatem scripto significat: 'ante ipse sufficiebam scribendis epistulis amicorum, nunc occupatissimus et infirmus Horatium nostrum a te cupio abducere. Veniet ergo ab ista parasitica mensa ad hanc regiam, et nos in epistulis scribendis adiuvabit.' Ac ne recusanti quidem aut succensuit quicquam aut amicitiam suam ingerere desiit. Exstant epistulae e quibus argumenti gratia pauca subieci: 'sume tibi aliquid iuris apud me, tanquam si convictor mihi fueris; recte enim et non temere feceris quoniam id usus mihi tecum esse volui, si per valetudinem tuam fieri possit.'...Praeterea saepe...homuncionem lepidissimum adpellat unaque et altera liberalitate locupletavit.' Horace had, in his later years, a house at Tibur, which was still shown in Suetonius' time. This is supposed to have been presented to him by Augustus.

[3] *Epist.* I. 20. 24, 25 (*corporis exigui, praecanum, solibus aptum,* | *irasci celerem, tamen ut placabilis essem*).

is given in *Sat.* I. 6 and II. 6. He suffered from dyspepsia and gout or rheumatism, which caused fits of despondency (*Epist.* I. 7 and 8). Even without this information about his health, we might easily infer from his poems that he was not a man of a hearty and energetic temperament.

Of the other Augustan poets in whom we are most interested, Horace certainly knew and loved and admired Vergil by far the best (see esp. *C.* I. 3). He was perhaps familiar with Tibullus (see *C.* I. 33 and *Epist.* I. 4), though Tibullus belonged to the literary circle of Messalla, not to that of Maecenas. He must have known and frequently met Propertius, who was another of Maecenas' *protégés*, but for some reason there was no love lost between the two men. Neither mentions the other, but, if Propertius was not the poet whose impertinence is described in *Sat.* I. 9, it is pretty clear that he was the poet whose vanity is criticised in *Epist.* II. 2. 87 sqq. (See Postgate, *Select Elegies* of Prop. p. xxxii.) Ovid, who was a friend of Propertius, once actually rebukes Horace (*A. A.* II. 271) and omits him from the list of entertaining poets (*A. A.* III. 329—340), though he pays him a tardy compliment after his death (*Trist.* IV. 10. 49).

§ 2. *Chronology of the Odes.*

It is generally believed, though it is hardly certain, that the first three books of the Odes were published together. Suetonius (*supra* p. xiv *n.*) says only that Augustus required Horace to add a fourth book long after the previous three had been published. But internal evidence is strongly in favour of the received opinion. Thus (1) the first ode of the series (I. 1) is addressed to Maecenas, the last but one (III. 29) is also addressed to Maecenas, and the last (III. 30) is a sort of *envoi*, the poet congratulating himself upon his own achievement. The first book of the Epistles is constructed on just this plan. The first letter and the last but one are addressed to Maecenas, the last is a humorous farewell, committing the book to the world. (2) No ode in the first three Books points clearly to a later date than B.C. 24. On the other hand, there are odes in all three Books which refer to this and earlier dates. Thus III. 14 relates to the return of Augustus from Spain: I. 24 to the death of Quintilius: and I. 29 to the expedition of Aelius Gallus into Arabia. All these events happened in B.C. 24. II. 4 was written near the end of Horace's fortieth year, i.e. B.C. 25. I. 31, II. 15 and III. 6 seem all to refer to the restoration of temples which occupied Augustus in B.C. 28. It is obvious that these odes could have been published together. (3) The first Book cannot have been published before B.C. 24, for it refers, as we have just seen, to events of that year. If the second and third Books were written (in part) and published later, why does Horace, about B.C. 20 (see *Epist.* I. 1. 1—10), speak as if he had long given up the practice of writing lyrics and could not resume it?

If, then, we assume that the first three Books were published together, they must have been published late in B.C. 24 or early in B.C. 23. This date is inferred from the fact that Marcellus, the nephew and adopted son of Augustus, is referred to as the hope of the Caesarian house in *Carm.* I. 12. 45—48; and Licinius Murena, brother-in-law of Maecenas, is addressed in *Carm.* II. 10 and referred to as living in III. 19. Marcellus died in the autumn of B.C. 23, and Murena was executed for conspiracy in B.C. 22. It is not likely that Horace published these references to them after their deaths.

The only other dates proposed are B.C. 19 and B.C. 22. The former date is suggested because I. 3 is supposed to refer to the voyage which Vergil took, to Greece, early in B.C. 19; and other odes, especially II. 9, are thought to refer to the expedition into Armenia of B.C. 20. The date of II. 9, however, seems to be fixed to the end of B.C. 25, or the beginning of 24, by the allusion to *tropaea Augusti Caesaris*, a grand monument so called, voted by the Senate in B.C. 25. (See the concluding note on II. 9.) As to I. 3, it is likely that this ode does not refer to Vergil's last voyage to Greece, for it says nothing about Vergil's ill-health.

The date B.C. 22 was proposed by the late Prof. Sellar because, in Epist. I. 13, Horace, who was sending his odes to Augustus, directs the messenger (one Vinnius Asina) to push on over hills, rivers and bogs, as if Augustus were far away at the time. Prof. Sellar guessed that Augustus was in Sicily or Asia, whither he went in B.C. 22. It is just as likely, however, that Augustus was at Gabii, undergoing the cold-water treatment which cured him of a grave illness in B.C. 23.

(*b*) *The Fourth Book*. The fourth book of the Odes was beyond question written some years after the first three. The opening ode itself, the language of *Epist*. I. 1. 1—10, and the express evidence of Suetonius (see p. xiv and *n.*) show that, after the publication of the first three Books, Horace had meant to abandon lyric composition, and only resumed it with reluctance. In the first ode, Horace describes himself as near 50 years of age. Odes 4 and 14 cannot have been written before the winter of B.C. 15, for they celebrate the grand campaign of that year in which Drusus conquered the Vindelici, Tiberius the Raeti. Ode 5 must have been written about the same time, for it complains of the long absence of Augustus, who had gone to Gaul in B.C. 16. Ode 2, perhaps, is a little later, for it was written when Augustus seemed likely to return to Rome soon. As a matter of fact, Augustus returned in July B.C. 13. It seems probable therefore that the book was published in B.C. 14 or early in 13. (On the metrical peculiarities of Book IV. see *infra* pp. xxviii, xxix and the first note to *C*. IV.)

§ 3. *Some Characteristics of Horace's Poetry*.

The Odes of Horace are avowedly imitations of Greek models: but there were Greek models of two quite different kinds, and Horace sometimes imitated them both at the same time. On the one hand, there were *public* odes, such as Pindar (B.C. 480) wrote—dithyrambs, paeans, songs of victory and dirges—solemn and elaborate compositions, intended to be sung by a trained chorus who danced or marched while they sang. On the other hand, there were lyrics such as Alcaeus or

Sappho or Anacreon wrote—songs intended to be sung by one person in a private circle[1].

The lyrics of Horace (though they were meant to be read or recited, not sung) belong entirely in form, and usually in substance, to the latter class. His metres are all borrowed from the Greek song-writers, and his Muse, as he often says, was inclined to be sportive (*iocosa*) rather than solemn[2]. Even in the *Carmen Saeculare* and in *Carm.* IV. 6, which were written for public performance by a chorus, he did not attempt the grand Pindaric elaboration which, he confesses indeed (*Carm.* IV. 2. 25—32), was beyond him. Yet several of the longer and graver odes (see especially III. 3, 4, 5, 11, 27, IV. 4), though still written in song-metres, are quite Pindaric in the treatment of the theme. In III. 3, for instance, the opening truism, the illustrations from many myths, the elaborate invention of Juno's compact and the brief sententious close are all clear imitations of Pindar[3]. The Pindaric tendency, here

[1] *Ars Poet.* 83—85. *Musa dedit fidibus divos puerosque deorum | et pugilem victorem et equum certamine primum | et iuvenum curas et libera vina referre.* Of these lines the first two refer to choral odes, and the third to songs. Lyrical poetry intended for a chorus is sometimes called *melic*.

[2] See *Carm.* I. 6: II. 1. 37 and 12. 1—5, 12—16: III. 3. 69: IV. 2 and 15.

[3] The extant odes of Pindar are all 'epinikia,' i.e. celebrations of the victories of certain persons in the great athletic contests of Greece. The following summary of the First Olympian Ode will sufficiently show Pindar's manner of treating a theme:

1—15. Water is the best drink: gold the choicest metal: so are the Olympic games the noblest games.

15—38. Let us sing the praises of Hiero, the victor, who won glory at Olympia, the home of Pelops.

38—55. Song can give currency to falsehoods, but we must not speak evil of deities.

56—85. Poseidon, of his great love, carried off Pelops. The tale that Pelops was killed and eaten is a base invention.

86—150. Because of the misdeeds of his father Tantalus, Pelops

conspicuously seen, to wander into mythology may be noticed
too in many of the shorter pieces (e.g. *Carm.* I. 7, 18: II. 4, 13:
III. 17: IV. 6). It should be remembered, however, that, in an
ode of Pindar, composed for a religious and patriotic festival, a
fine local myth, showing forth 'the glories of our birth and
state,' was especially appropriate; and that moralizing too was,
in Pindar's day, as much expected of the poet as fine images
and musical rhythms. He was the popular philosopher, the
seer who could discern the tendencies of men's actions and
could pronounce upon them with due blame or praise.

Horace derived, then, from his Greek models a certain
discursiveness in his treatment of a theme. He took from
them also an extreme 'abruptness' of manner, such that it is
often difficult to follow the train of his thoughts (see, for
instance, I. 7 or II. 2 or III. 4 or IV. 9). This abruptness is due
partly to the brevity of his diction and partly to a literary convention. As the poet Gray wrote to his friend Mason, 'extreme
conciseness of expression, yet pure, perspicuous and musical, is
one of the great beauties of lyric poetry.' And the reason is
obvious. In short lines, with a marked rhythmical beat, almost
every word becomes emphatic and must deserve to be emphatic.
This conciseness necessarily leads to abruptness of thought, for
the conjunctions and brief explanatory phrases which, in a freer
style of composition, serve to mark the connexion of ideas,
are excluded from lyrics by their unemphatic character. It is a
convention also, between poets and their audience, that lyrics,
however elaborate, should profess to be written on the inspiration of the moment, and should therefore seem to be hurried,
unpremeditated, unmethodical. They are spoilt if they become
argumentative.

In real inspiration Horace was probably deficient. Certainly

was sent back to earth and, by help of Poseidon, he won Hippodamia
to wife in a chariot-race at Olympia.

150—160. From that time forth the glory of the Olympian races
has shone abroad.

161—184. I sing the victor, Hiero, wisest and greatest of kings.
Win again, Hiero, and be thou first among kings, I among poets.

his poems are not, to use Wordsworth's phrase, 'the sponta-
neous overflow of powerful feeling.' He himself describes them
as laborious (*operosa carmina C.* IV. 2. 31). But they are sincere,
that is to say, they are the genuine expression of his thoughts and
sentiments ; and if they do not reveal to us a man of profound
insight or ardent passions or lofty imagination, they show at
least sympathy, affection, humour, a generous admiration of
great men and noble deeds, and a sturdy pride in his vocation.
And a man with these qualities, if his vocation happens to be
literature, has always been sure of a lasting success. The tact
which results from his sympathy and humour appears in his
style as well as in his matter, and his writings have the charm
which is recognized as 'companionable.' In our own country,
Addison and Lamb, in France, Montaigne and Mme. de
Sévigné, are conspicuous examples of the Horatian temperament and of its enduring popularity. And Horace had the
advantage of writing in verse and of using a language which
gave the utmost assistance to his special literary talent. 'The
best words in the best places' is a definition of poetry that
Coleridge was fond of repeating. It might serve for a description of Horace's writing. He was gifted by nature with a fine
ear and an infinite capacity for taking pains, and he had had
a scholarly education. He borrowed, from Greek, metres of
peculiar swing, and he had, in his native Latin, a store of
sonorous and pregnant words, a terse and lucid grammar, and
the liberty to arrange his words to the best advantage. With
these resources, he has produced an incomparable series of
brilliant phrases ('jewels five words long' Tennyson calls them)
which are at once easy to remember and impossible to translate[1].

[1] It is idle to quote instances where almost every line is an instance,
but one might choose *simplex munditiis* or *insaniens sapientia* or
splendide mendax as examples of Horace's untranslateable brevity :
dulce et decorum est pro patria mori or *nihil est ab omni parte beatum* as
examples of finished commonplace: *non indecoro pulvere sordidos* or
intaminatis fulget honoribus or *impavidum ferient ruinae* as specimens
of sonority, and *qui fragilem truci commisit pelago ratem* as an instance
of the artful arrangement of contrasted words.

To a writer with this faculty, it matters little that his ideas are scanty and commonplace. His readers have the less trouble in understanding him and agreeing with him, and can surrender themselves to the charm of his diction. It is because we all find in Horace 'what oft was thought but ne'er so well express'd' that he has been used, for so many ages, as the indispensable model of literary excellence.

§ 4. *Some Characteristics of Horace's Latinity.*

Horace's Latin is a good deal affected by the conciseness which, as we have just said (p. xx) was demanded by the perpetually recurring emphases of lyric poetry. For the sake of brevity he often used expressions which may be called 'short cuts,' intended to avoid unemphatic prepositions and conjunctions, and to bring important words closer together. The most striking instances of this practice are his use of the genitive case and of the infinitive mood. His freedom in the use of these constructions was undoubtedly imitated from the Greek, though it is not always possible to produce a Greek parallel for every Horatian instance.

1. The following are examples, in the Odes, of unusual genitives: *diva potens Cypri* (I. 3. 1), *agrestium regnavit populorum* (III. 30. 11), *desine querelarum* (II. 9. 17, 18), *abstineto irarum* (III. 27. 69, 70), *integer vitae scelerisque purus* (I. 22. 1), *patriae exul* (II. 16. 19), *prosperam frugum* (IV. 6. 39), *fertilis frugum* (*Carm. Saec.* 29), *fecunda culpae* (III. 6. 17), *pauper aquae* (III. 30. 11), *dives artium* (IV. 8. 5), *docilis modorum* (IV. 6. 43), probably also *notus animi paterni* (II. 2. 6, though these words need not be construed together)[1].

2. The infinitive mood is often used by Horace, as it is often used in Greek, where in prose a final or a consecutive

---

[1] The Greek constructions imitated are such as βασιλεύειν Πύλου, λήγειν ἀοιδῆς, ἀγνὸς αἵματος, φυγὰς Ἄργους, πλούσιος χρυσίου, μαθητικὸς μουσικῆς, θαυμάζειν τινὰ τοῦ νοῦ.

clause (with *ut* and the subj.) would be required[1]. Some of the instances in Horace (e.g. *certat tollere* in I. 1. 6, or *gaudet posuisse* I. 34. 16, or *tendentes imposuisse* III. 4. 52) can be paralleled in prose, but the following are extremely bold : *pecus egit visere* (I. 2. 8), *coniurata rumpere* and *furit reperire* (I. 15. 7 and 27), *te persequor frangere* (I. 23. 10), *tradam ventis portare* (I. 26. 3), *laborat trepidare* (II. 3. 11), *urges summovere* (II. 18. 21), *dedit spernere* (II. 16. 39), *impulerit maturare necem* (III. 7. 14—16), *me expetit urere* (*Epod.* 11. 5).

The infinitive is similarly used with adjectives to suggest a purpose or consequence, or to limit the aspect of the epithet[2] : as *indocilis pati* (I. 1. 18), *callidus condere* (I. 10. 7), *blandus ducere* I. 12. 11, 12), *praesens tollere* and *dolosus ferre* (I. 35. 2 and 28), *leviora tolli* (II. 4. 11), *pertinax ludere* (III. 29. 53), *efficax eluere* (IV. 12. 20), *veraces cecinisse* (Carm. Saec. 25), *lubricus aspici* (I. 19. 8), *niveus videri* (IV. 2. 59), *nefas videre* (Epod. 16. 14), *nobilis superare* (I. 12. 26), and *dolens vinci* (IV. 4. 62.)

It is obvious that, in many of these instances, a gerund with or without a preposition might have been used. Horace, however, regards the infinitive (in the Greek way) as an indeclinable noun.

These constructions, though found in other Latin poets, are specially characteristic of Horace ; but, besides these, he has many other and more common devices to procure that perpetual quaintness which, as Aristotle said, is essential to poetical diction.

3. With adjectives, he is partial to a kind of *hypallage*

---

[1] The Greek constructions imitated are such as ἀνὴρ χαλεπὸς συζῆν, παρέχω ἐμαυτὸν τῷ ἰατρῷ τέμνειν, θαῦμα ἰδέσθαι, λευκὸς ὁρᾶσθαι.

[2] In the instances above cited, grammarians would call some of the infinitives *prolate* or *complementary*, others *epexegetical* or *explanatory*. The difference between the two kinds is briefly this: the prolate infin. is necessary to limit the meaning of the preceding verb or adjective, while the epexegetical infin. is merely illustrative of the meaning. E.g. *celer irasci* means 'quick to anger,' not 'quick at everything, anger included,' whereas *blandus ducere quercus* does mean ' persuasive to everything, oaks included.'

(i.e. 'inversion of relations'), whereby an epithet is transferred from the producer to the thing produced or vice versa.

Of the first case, *iracunda fulmina* (I. 3. 40), *dementes ruinas* (I. 37. 7), *iratos apices* (III. 21. 19), *invido flatu* (IV. 5. 9), are good enough examples. Instances of the second case are more interesting, because here the meaning of the adjective is somewhat affected. Thus *nigri venti* (I. 5. 7) means, in effect, 'blackening winds,' and *albus* (I. 7. 15) or *candidus* (III. 7. 1), applied to a wind, means 'clearing,' 'brightening.' Similar examples are *palma nobilis* (I. 1. 5), *decorae palaestrae* (I. 10. 4), *insigni Camena* (I. 12. 39), *inaequales procellae* (II. 9. 3), *informes hiemes* (II. 10. 5).

Horace is somewhat free in his use of adjectives in *-bilis* or *-ilis*. Thus *flebilis* (I. 24. 9), *amabilis* (II. 9. 13), *docilis* (III. 11. 1 and IV. 6. 43), are equivalent to *defletus, amatus, doctus*. On the other hand, passive participles, such as *irruptus* (I. 13. 18), *indomitus* (II. 14. 2), *intaminatus* (III. 2. 18), often supply the place of an adjective in *-bilis*.

4. The neuter sing. of an adjective is sometimes used as an adverb : as *dulce ridentem* (I. 22. 23), *lucidum fulgentes* (II. 12. 14), *perfidum ridens* (III. 27. 67), *turbidum laetatur* (II. 19. 6).

5. A few words not used elsewhere (ἅπαξ λεγόμενα) occur in the Odes. Such are *inaudax* (III. 20. 3), *exultim* (III. 11. 10), *immetatus* (III. 24. 12), *Faustitas* (IV. 5. 18), *inemori* (Epod. 5. 34).

6. The dative case is many times used for *in* with accus. after a verb of sending : e.g. *terris misit* (I. 2. 1), *mittes lucis* (I. 12. 60), *compulerit gregi* (I. 24. 18), *caelo tuleris* (III. 23. 1), and a similar use may be suspected elsewhere (*e.g. C.* II. 7. 16, IV. 1. 7).

7. Of strange ablatives *Cecropio cothurno* in II. 1. 12 and *coniuge barbara* in III. 5. 5 are conspicuous instances. Abl. of the agent without *ab* occurs perhaps in I. 6. 1 (where see note).

8. Certain oddities in the arrangement of words may also be noticed.

(*a*) An epithet, really qualifying two words, is often put with the second only. E.g. in I. 2. 1 *nivis atque dirae grandinis* : 5. 5 *fidem mutatosque deos* : also I. 31. 16 : 34. 8 : II. 8. 3 : 19. 24 : III. 2. 16 : 11. 39 : IV. 14. 4.

(*b*) Similarly, a verb, which belongs to both parts of a compound sentence, is often inserted in the second part with *-que* or *-ve*: e.g. I. 30. 6 *Gratiae properentque nymphae*: II. 7. 24 *apio curatve myrto.* Also II. 17. 16 : 19. 28, 31 : III. 4. 12 : *Carm. Saec.* 22.

(*c*) Sentences in which a word may be constructed with either of two other words—the so-called construction ἀπὸ κοινοῦ or 'in common'—are frequent. A striking instance is in II. 18. 37 *hic levare functum* | *pauperem laboribus* | *vocatus atque non vocatus audit.* Here *laboribus* is appropriate to *levare* and to *functum* : and *levare* is appropriate to *vocatus* and to *audit.* So in II. 11. 11 *consiliis* may be constructed with *minorem* and *fatigas* : and in III. 8. 19 *sibi* with *infestus* or *dissidet.*

That the Romans found something inimitable in Horace's style is evident from the rarity and badness of the attempts to imitate him. The few pieces of sapphics and alcaics in Statius and Ausonius are almost doggrel.

§ 5. *Metres of the Odes.*

The first eleven odes of the 1st Book comprise examples of nearly all the metres used by Horace in the Odes. The only novelties introduced in later books are the Hipponactic stanza of II. 18, the Archilochian of IV. 7 and the Ionic of III. 12.

Metre, in Latin and Greek, is the arrangement of long and short syllables in a line of poetry.

Rhythm is the arrangement of stresses (*ictus*) or loud syllables. In other words, metre is the mode of constructing a line : rhythm is the mode of reading or singing it [1].

For purposes of metre, all long syllables are alike, and all short syllables are alike : but for purposes of rhythm (as in music) long syllables may be of different lengths, and short syllables may be of different lengths.

---

[1] In English metre and rhythm are identical, for with us a syllable which has stress is long, and a syllable which has no stress is short.

In Horace's Odes, we know the metres, but we do not know the rhythms. In other words we do not know how Horace himself would have read and scanned his lines. For instance, the First Ode of the First Book consists of lines of this metre: $---\cup\cup--\cup\cup-\cup\bar\cup$. But the lines may be scanned and read in several different ways: thus

(1) Maéce | nás ata | vís | édite | régi | bús.

(2) Maéce | nás atavis | édite reg | ibús.

(3) Maéce | nás ata | vís | édite | régibus.

(4) Maécenas at | avís edi | te régibus.

Of these methods, the first represents the original Greek rhythm : the second, the scansion which was adopted by grammarians nearly contemporary with Horace: the third, a possible scansion which occurs naturally to an English reader : the fourth is an old-fashioned method which is seldom mentioned now, but which has some merits.

That Horace usually employed the second method, is rendered probable by such lines as

       exegi monumentum aere perennius   (III. 30. 1)

or   *perrupit Acheronta Herculeus labor*   (I. 3. 36) :

still more by such a line as

       dum flagrantia detorquet ad oscula   (II. 12. 25).

These instances suggest that there was not such a pause on the sixth syllable as is required by the first method or the third.

But it would seem that, in this matter of 'pause,' Horace was not likely to be consistent. Witness his treatment of *synapheia.*

Synapheia is the 'connexion' of line with line, so that (among other effects) a syllable liable to elision may not conclude a line if the next line begins with a vowel. Horace, as a rule, follows the Greek lyrists in maintaining synapheia, and several times elides a concluding syllable before a vowel at the beginning of the next line, or divides a word between two lines. See, for elision, II. 2. 11 : 3. 27 : 16. 34 : III. 29. 35 : IV. 1. 35 : 2. 22 and 23: *Carm. Saec.* 47 : and, for division, I. 2. 19: 25. 11 : II. 16. 7. But in I. 2. 41 and 47: I. 8. 3: I. 12. 6 and 7, and many other places, synapheia is ignored and hiatus permitted. Hiatus, of course, implies a slight pause, while synapheia implies that there was no pause between two lines.

For reasons such as these, it is impossible to put forward an authoritative scansion to Horace's lines. In the metrical schemes here subjoined no scansion will be suggested, but the original (i.e. the Greek) rhythm will be given in musical notation according to the theories of Dr J. H. H. Schmidt[1]. It will be seen that Dr Schmidt divides a line into bars of equal length, i.e. occupying the same time in delivery.

In the metrical schemes, a comma marks the caesura or diaeresis, i.e. the point which must coincide with the end of a word[2].

It remains to be added that all the odes of Horace seem to be divisible into stanzas of four lines. The only exceptions are IV. 8, which there are many reasons for rejecting in whole or in part: and III. 12, which consists of four periods of ten feet each. The metres were undoubtedly borrowed by Horace from the Greek lyrists, especially Alcaeus, but he has introduced many small alterations, such as the use of long syllables where the Greeks allowed shorts, and the regular use of caesura where the Greeks had none.

I. The **Alcaic** stanza is used in 37 odes, viz.:

I. 9. 16. 17. 26. 27. 29. 31. 34. 35. 37.

II. 1. 3. 5. 7. 9. 11. 13. 14. 15. 17. 19. 20.

III. 1. 2. 3. 4. 5. 6. 17. 21. 23. 26. 29.

IV. 4. 9. 14. 15.

---

[1] *Rhythmic and Metric of the Classical Languages*, translated by Dr J. W. White.

[2] Technically, *caesura* is the division of a foot between two words, so that part of the foot belongs to one word, the remainder to another. *Diaeresis*, on the other hand, is the division of feet from one another so that one foot ends with a word, while the next begins a new word. Thus, in the bucolic hexameter, there is caesura in the third foot and diaeresis between the fourth and fifth : as

Nos patri | ae fi | nes et | dulcia | linquimus | arva.

The metrical scheme is :

I, 2. ⏒ – ‿ – –, – ‿ ‿ – ‿ ⏒ (eleven syllables).

3. ⏒ – ‿ – – – ‿ – ⏒ (nine syllables).

4. – ‿ ‿ – ‿ ‿ – ‿ – ⏒ (ten syllables).

The first two lines begin with a short syllable only 18 times (out of 634 examples)[1].

The diaeresis (which was not used by the Greeks) after the fifth syllable is neglected in I. 16. 21 : 37. 5 : 37. 14 : II. 17. 21 : IV. 14. 17. Elision occurs at the diaeresis in III. I. 5 : 4. 49. The fifth syllable is short in III. 5. 17 : and possibly III. 23. 18.

In the third line, the first syllable is short only 10 times in 317 examples. The fifth syllable is, in Horace, always long, though in Alcaeus it appears to have been always short. A most important rule in the construction of this line is that it shall not end with two dissyllabic words. Such an ending occurs only 8 times, viz. I. 16. 4 : 26. 7 : 29. 11 : II. I. 11 : 13. 27 : 14. 11 : 19. 7 : 19. 11 : and in 5 of these eight instances, the first dissyllable is repeated at the beginning of the next line (e.g. II. 13. 27 *dura navis | dura fugae mala*).

In the fourth line, there is usually caesura after the fourth syllable, but the main rule is that the line shall not begin with two trisyllabic words (e.g. *tristia tempora*).

Synapheia of the third and fourth lines occurs in II. 3. 27 : III. 29. 35, but is conspicuously neglected in I. 16. 27 : 17. 13 : II. 13. 7. Yet, on the whole, synapheia is usually respected. 'An Alcaic line does not often end with a short vowel, even when the next line begins with a consonant.' (Ramsay, *Latin Prosody*, p. 212.)

The original rhythm, according to Dr Schmidt, was :

---

[1] In the IVth Book, the opening syllable is always long.

This rhythm is trochaic, with an *anacrusis* (or 'striking-up' syllable) at the beginning of lines 1, 2, 3.

2. The Sapphic stanza is used in 25 odes, viz.:

I. 2. 10. 12. 20. 22. 25. 30. 32. 38.
II. 2. 4. 6. 8. 10. 16.
III. 8. 11. 14. 18. 20. 22. 27.
IV. 2. 6. 11 and *Carmen Saeculare*.

The stanza seems to have been invented by Alcaeus, though it is named after Sappho. The metrical scheme is:

1, 2, 3. $-\cup--- , \cup\cup-\cup-\breve{\upsilon}$ (eleven syllables).
4. $-\cup\cup-\breve{\upsilon}$ (five syllables).

The longer line is called *the lesser Sapphic:* the shorter the *Adonius*.

In the longer line Horace always has the fourth syllable long, whereas Sappho (and Catullus) often had it short.

Horace has also introduced a caesura, which was not used by Sappho. This caesura, in the first three Books, generally occurs after the 5th syllable, and only occasionally after the 6th (e.g. I. 10. 1, 6, 18), but in the fourth Book and *Carm. Saec.* it is very frequently placed after the 6th syllable (in fact, 39 times in only four compositions).

Synapheia is obviously respected between the 2nd and 3rd lines in II. 2. 18: 16. 34: IV. 2. 22; where final syllables are elided: and between the 3rd and 4th lines in I. 2. 19: 25. 11: II. 16. 7: IV. 2. 23: *Carm. Saec.* 47, where either a word is divided (as in the first three passages) or a syllable elided (as in the last two).

Yet hiatus between the lines frequently occurs, as in I. 2. 41 and 47: 12. 6 and 7 etc.

The original rhythm, according to Dr Schmidt, was trochaic and may be represented thus:

3. A stanza called the *Greater Sapphic* is used in I. 8. It consists of couplets of the following form:

1, 3. $-\cup\cup-\cup-\overline{\cup}$.

2, 4. $-\cup---, \cup\cup-, -\cup\cup-\cup-\overset{\smile}{-}$.

It will be seen that the first line is longer by two syllables than the Adonius, and the second line is longer by four $(-\cup\cup-)$ than the lesser Sapphic.

The original rhythm is said to be:

4. The metres called **Asclepiad** are founded on the following lines:

(*a*) $---\cup\cup-, -\cup\cup-\cup\overset{\smile}{-}$ ('lesser Asclepiad').

(*b*) $---\cup\cup-, -\cup\cup-, -\cup\cup-\cup\overset{\smile}{-}$ ('greater Asclepiad').

(*c*) $---\cup\cup-\cup\overset{\smile}{-}$ ('Glyconic').

(*d*) $---\cup\cup--$ ('Pherecratic').

In the Lesser Asclepiad, the caesura is neglected in II. 12. 25 and IV. 8. 17. A short syllable is lengthened at the caesura in I. 13. 6: III. 16. 26.

In the Greater Asclepiad there are two caesuras, but the second is neglected in I. 18. 16.

In the Glyconic, the second syllable is perhaps short in I. 15. 24 and 36.

These lines are combined by Horace into four-line stanzas of different kinds thus:

(A) The *First Asclepiad* stanza employs (*a*) alone. See I. I, III. 30, IV. 8.

(B) The *Second Asclepiad* has (*b*) alone. See I. 11 and 18: IV. 10.

(C) The *Third Asclepiad* has couplets of (*a*) and (*c*). See I. 3. 13. 19. 36. III. 9. 15. 19. 24. 25. 28. IV. 1. 3.

(D) The *Fourth Asclepiad* has (*a*) thrice repeated, followed by (*c*). See I. 6. 15. 24. 33. II. 12. III. 10. 16. IV. 5. 12.

(E) The *Fifth Asclepiad* has (*a*) twice repeated, then (*d*), then (*c*). See I. 5. 14. 21. 23. III. 7. 13. IV. 13.

The original rhythms are said to be:

(a)
(b)
(c)
(d)

5. The *Alcmanian* stanza is used in I. 7 and 28, and in Epode 12. It consists of couplets made up of an ordinary dactylic hexameter, followed by a dactylic tetrameter.

1, 3. $-\smile\smile\ |-\smile\smile\ |-,\ \smile\smile\ |-\smile\smile\ |-\smile\smile\ |-\underline{\smile}.$

2, 4. $-\smile\smile\ |-\smile\smile\ |-\smile\smile\ |-\underline{\smile}.$

In the second line, there is usually a caesura in the second or third dactyl.

The rhythm is really dactylic, i.e. each dactyl is of the value and each spondee of the value .

6. The other metres used in the Odes are exhibited only in single specimens, which are treated in the notes as they severally occur (see II. 18. III. 12. IV. 7). But the metre of I. 4 may be specially noticed here.

It is called the *Fourth Archilochian*, and consists of a four-line stanza in which the lines are arranged as follows:

1, 3. $-\smile\smile\ -\smile\smile\ -,\ \smile\smile\ -\smile\smile,\ -\smile-\smile--.$

2, 4. $\smile-\smile-\smile,\ -\smile-\smile--.$

The first line is called 'the greater Archilochian': the second is an 'iambic trimeter catalectic'[1].

This combination is so curious that Dr Schmidt thinks that Horace must have read the dactyls as , not as , so that the rhythm becomes trochaic, thus:

1, 3.
2, 4.

[1] A 'catalectic,' or 'stopping' line, is one which comes to an end in the middle of a foot.

§ 6. *Order of the Odes.*

Though there is some reason to suspect slight interpolations in the Odes (see below, p. xxxiv), there is no reason for doubting that the present arrangement of the poems is substantially that of Horace himself. But the order is clearly not chronological: e.g. I. 24 was written in B.C. 24, while III. 1—6 were written in B.C. 27. Nor are poems of one kind, either in subject or metre, placed together, for (e.g.) political poems and Alcaic odes occur in all parts of the collection.

But we can often discern special reasons for placing single odes or groups of odes in particular places. Thus I. 1, II. 20, III. 29 and 30, IV. 1, are obviously appropriate to their places: the six great odes at the beginning of Book III. form a definite cycle, and it is not an accident that the first nine odes of Book I. are specimens of nearly all the metres that Horace attempted, or that the first three odes are addressed to Maecenas, Augustus and Vergil.

In regard to the bulk of the poems, however, it is likely that Horace deliberately threw them into some confusion in order to favour that appearance of inspiration and unpremeditatedness which, as was noticed above (p. xx), was one of the conventions of lyrical composition. His Muse, he would have us believe, was a whimsical lady, but we may say of her, as Congreve said of Fair Amoret,

> "Careless she is with artful care,
> Affecting to seem unaffected."

One noticeable device for securing this effect was to place in juxtaposition odes written in different moods, the grave with the gay, the lively with the severe (e.g. I. 12 and 13, 24 and 25, 37 and 38: II. 3 and 4: III. 6 and 7). Another is to pretend that the casual thought of one ode suggested the whole theme of the next, as the mention of Fortune in I. 34 suggests I. 35, and the mention of a holiday in III. 17 suggests III. 18. Contrasts of subject too are not infrequent, as where in II. 6 and 7 the quiet

stay-at-home life of Horace gives extra point to his welcome of
the wanderer Pompeius: and in III. 23 and 24 the praise of
simple piety leads up to a denunciation of wealth.

§ 7.   *The Text.*

Horace's works, as he himself prophesied (*Epist.* I. 20. 17,
18), soon became one of the regular Roman schoolbooks. They
were so in the time of Quintilian and Juvenal (say A.D. 100), and
remained so in the time of Ausonius (say A.D. 380). Vergil, too,
shared the same fate (see Mayor's note on Juvenal VII. 227).
But while of Vergil we have several MSS. complete or fragmentary, which date from a very high antiquity (earlier than A.D.
500), we have only one of Horace which is as old as the 9th
century. Most of the extant MSS. of Horace were written in
the 10th century or later.

Moreover, no extant MS. of Horace seems to have been
written in Italy. The oldest, called B (*Bernensis,* of the 9th
century), is a fragmentary copy written in Ireland. The others
appear to have been all written in France or Germany after that
revival of schools and of literary studies which Charlemagne
introduced with the assistance of Alcuin of York (about A.D.
820). There is evidence that Horace was well known to some
students at this time, though many years must have elapsed
before the reading of profane poets was permitted in the
cathedral schools of the German Empire. At Paderborn, for
instance, it was not till after A.D. 1000 that it could be said
'viguit *Horatius,* magnus et *Virgilius, Crispus* ac *Salustius* et
Urbanus Statius.' (See Maitland's *Dark Ages,* Nos. XI. and
VIII. and *Class. Review* 1894, p. 305.)

Of the extant MSS., other than B, the chief are Aφψλπ, all
now at Paris: δ and *d,* both in the British Museum: R, now in
the Vatican (though it was written in Alsace): *l* at Leyden: *a*
at Milan: ν at Dessau. All these, with some others, are
assigned to the 10th century, and there are many more of later
date.

Most of the oldest MSS. have been inspected by more than one editor, but the fullest collation will be found in the editions of O. Keller and A. Holder (see esp. their *editio minor* of 1879).

The text of Horace presented in these MSS. is not in a satisfactory state: that is to say, it leaves grave doubt, in very many places, as to what Horace really wrote. Apart from the numerous passages where we have two alternative readings, both good (see next page), there are places where there are alternatives both bad (e.g. III. 4. 10 *limen Apuliae*, or III. 24. 4 *mare Apulicum*, or Epod. 9. 17 *ad hunc*), and places where the MSS. are agreed but the reading can hardly be sound (e.g. I. 20. 10 *bibes*, I. 23. 5 *veris adventus*, II. 2. 2 *inimice*, III. 26. 7 *arcus*, IV. 2. 49 *teque*). And there are many places, too, where interpolation may reasonably be suspected: such as I. 31. 13—16, III. 11. 17—20, and IV. 8 (either the whole or part). In this matter it should be remembered that epigrams were interpolated in Martial's works in his own life-time (as he himself complains, e.g. I. 54, X. 100), and that Horace, being a schoolbook, was especially liable to interpolation. A good schoolmaster, for instance, in commenting on Horace's style, would doubtless compose a stanza now and again, to show the trick of it, and some of these imitations, written in the margin of the text, with other notes for lessons, might easily pass into the text itself[1].

The question, however, whether a certain stanza is interpolated, or a certain reading is good enough for Horace, must always remain open, unless some more authoritative MS. is discovered. But the existing MSS. undoubtedly prove that the text of Horace was, in very ancient times, doubtful, and was emended by good scholars. A considerable number of our

---

[1] It is observable, here, that in the Appendix on prosody to the *Ars Grammatica* of Diomedes, a grammarian of the 4th century, only 35 Odes are ascribed to Bk. I. (omitting 22, 25, 35): only 19 to Bk. II. (omitting 16), and only 25 to Bk. III. The Harleian MS. No. 2724, in the British Museum, has at the end some Sapphics beginning

Flante cum terram Zephyro solutam
Floribus vestit redimita terra.

MSS. contain, at the end of the Epodes, the following *sub-scriptio*:

Vettius Agorius Basilius Mavortius v. c. et inl. (vir consularis et inlustris) *ex com̃. dom̃.* (ex comite domestico) *ex coñs. or̃d.* (ex consule ordinario) *legi et ut potui emendavi conferente mihi Magistro Felice oratore urbis Romae.*

This Mavortius was consul A.D. 527, and probably edited both the odes and the epodes. Unfortunately, it is not possible to restore his edition even from the MSS. which bear his *sub-scriptio*, for these MSS. differ from one another at most of the crucial points. But it is plain that our copies are descended from two editions of Horace, that of Mavortius for one, and another of which we do not know the origin. These editions differed from one another in a great number of single words: e.g.

Carminum, I.	4.	8	*visit, urit.*
	18.	5	*increpat, crepat.*
	27.	13	*voluptas, voluntas.*
	28.	15	*mors, nox.*
	32.	1	*poscimus, poscimur.*
	35.	17	*saeva, serva.*
II.	3.	28	*exitium, exilium.*
	13.	8	*laborem, laborum.*
	20.	13	*ocior, notior.*
III.	3.	34	*ducere, discere.*
	5.	37	*aptius, inscius.*
	8.	27	*rape, cape.*
	14.	6	*divis, sacris.*
	15.	2	*fige, pone.*
	19.	27	*Rhode, Chloe.*
	23.	19	*mollivit, mollibit.*
	27.	48	*monstri, tauri.*
	29.	34	*aequore, alveo.*
IV.	2.	58	*ortum, orbem.*
	4.	36	*dedecorant, indecorant.*
	7.	17	*vitae, summae.*
	13.	14	*cari, clari.*
	14.	28	*meditatur, minitatur.*

Epodon,	2. 25	*ripis, rivis.*
	5. 15	*implicata, illigata.*
	5. 58	*suburanae, suburbanae.*
	16. 61	*astri, austri.*
	17. 11	*unxere, luxere.*
	17. 64	*laboribus, doloribus.*
Carmen Saeculare,	23	*totiens, totidem.*
	65	*arces, aras.*

In these instances (and many more might have been given) there is usually little to be said in favour of one reading and against the other, and the MSS. are very fairly divided between the two. But the MSS. which agree in one reading do not agree in the next, and very often indeed both readings together are recorded in the same MS.

One or two examples will illustrate the extreme perplexity of the authorities. In *C.* I. 2. 18 the absurd reading *jactat velorum* (for *ultorem*) appears in seven MSS. φψλlδzπ. It would naturally be supposed that these MSS. were derived from one source, but in I. 4. 8, λlπ read *urit* while φψδz read *visit* (which λl also record as a variant). In I. 9. 6 φψδπ have the absurd reading *largiri potis* for *large reponens*, but in 8. 2 δπ have *hoc deos oro*, while φψ have *te deos oro*. Again, only three MSS. λlu omit the line I. 5. 13, but 12. 26, which is also omitted in λl, is not omitted in *u*, but is omitted in δzπL. One is perpetually baffled by difficulties of this kind in attempting to trace the history and connexions of our MSS. It would seem that the monks, who wrote our copies, had more than one text before them, or one text smothered with notes and corrections, and as most of the copies were made about the same time, it is impossible to distinguish two or three of them as being the source, or as representing the source, of all the rest.

A very large body of marginal notes or *scholia* on Horace has come down to us. They are in the main derived from two commentaries on Horace, written by Pomponius Porphyrion and Helenius Acron. Porphyrion appears to have lived about A.D. 200, and Acron still earlier, for he is cited (on *Sat.* I. 8. 25) by Porphyrion. But the notes which we now have under the name of Acron were evidently put together by a writer who lived some time after the Roman Empire had adopted Christianity. These *scholia* are not of much assistance in the attempt to restore the words of Horace himself. Often they do not comment on the words in dispute and, when they do, Porphyrion often supports one reading, Acron the other. Sometimes, too, one reading is quoted as a heading to a note while the note itself explains the other. No editor has at present found the clue to all this tangle. Messrs Keller and Holder, who have examined far more MSS. than anybody else, have divided them into three classes, but the grounds on which they base this division are most unsatisfactory.

The chief editions of the text of Horace during the last 350 years are those of M. A. Muretus (Venice, 1551), D. Lambinus (Lyons, 1561), J. Cruquius (Antwerp, 1578), D. Heinsius (Leyden, 1605), T. Faber (Saumur, 1671), R. Bentley (Cambridge, 1711), C. Fea (Rome, 1811), F. Pottier (Paris, 1823), A. Meineke (Berlin, 1834), P. H. Peerlkamp (Haarlem, 1834), J. C. Orelli (Zurich, 1837), W. Dillenburger (Bonn, 1844), F. Ritter (Leipzig, 1856), K. Lehrs (Leipzig, 1859), H. A. J. Munro (Cambridge, 1869), O. Keller and A. Holder (ed. major, Leipzig, 1864—1870 and ed. minor, Leipzig, 1879). Among these, the edition of J. Cruquius is especially noteworthy because it is founded mainly on some MSS. (Blandinii) which formerly existed at Ghent (Blandenberg Abbey), but which were burnt in 1566 soon after Cruquius collated them. One of them, which editors call V (*vetustissimus*), was a very good MS., but not specially good in the odes. Fea used the MSS. now in Italy: Orelli those in Switzerland: Pottier those in Paris. Other editors have chosen MSS. in different libraries. Keller and Holder have inspected about 50 MSS. and have carefully collated about 25 in various countries.

The chief commentaries on Horace, at least in regard to the collection of illustrative matter, are those of Orelli and Dillenburger.

§ 8. *Imitations of Greek Poets.*

The following collection of fragments from Greek poets is taken from the edition of Horace by Keller and Häussner (Leipzig and Prague, 1885). It consists of passages which Horace seems to have imitated in thought or metre.

1. *C.* I. 1.—Pindari *frag.* 221 (ed. Bergk⁴).

..'Αελλοπόδων μέν τιν' εὐφραίνοισιν ἵππων
τίμια καὶ στέφανοι, τοὺς δ' ἐν πολυχρύσοις θαλάμοις βιοτά·
τέρπεται δὲ καί τις ἔπι (φρασὶν) οἶδμ' ἐνάλιον
ναῒ θοᾷ σῶς διαστείβων ...

2. *C.* I. 9.—Alcaei *fr.* 34.

Ὕει μὲν ὁ Ζεύς, ἐκ δ' ὀράνω μέγας
χείμων, πεπάγασιν δ' ὑδάτων ῥόαι.

— — — — —

κάββαλλε τὸν χείμων', ἐπὶ μὲν τίθεις
πῦρ, ἐν δὲ κίρναις οἶνον ἀφειδέως
μέλιχρον, αὐτὰρ ἀμφὶ κόρσᾳ
μάλθακον ἀμφι ... γνόφαλλον.

3. *C.* I. 10.—Alcaei *fr.* 5.

Χαῖρε Κυλλάνας ὁ μέδεις, σὲ γάρ μοι
θῦμος ὕμνην, τοι κορύφαις ἐν αὔταις
Μαῖα γέννατο Κρονίδᾳ μίγεισα.

4. *C.* I. 12.—Pindari *Olymp.* 2. 1 sq.

Ἀναξιφόρμιγγες ὕμνοι,
τίνα θεόν, τίν' ἥρωα, τίνα δ' ἄνδρα κελαδήσομεν;

5. *C.* I. 14.—Alcaei *fr.* 18.

Ἀσυνέτημι τῶν ἀνέμων στάσιν·
τὶ μὲν γὰρ ἔνθεν κῦμα κυλίνδεται,
τὸ δ' ἔνθεν· ἄμμες δ' ἀν τὸ μέσσον
ναῒ φορήμεθα σὺν μελαίνᾳ,
χείμωνι μοχθεῦντες μεγάλῳ μάλα·
περ μὲν γὰρ ἄντλος ἱστοπέδαν ἔχει,
λαῖφος δὲ πᾶν ζάδηλον ἤδη
καὶ λάκιδες μεγάλαι κατ' αὔτο·
χόλαισι δ' ἄγκοιναι.

6. *C.* I. 18.—Alcaei *fr.* 44.

Μηδὲν ἄλλο φυτεύσῃς πρότερον δένδριον ἀμπέλω.

7. *C.* I. 23.—Anacreontis *fr.* 51.

Ἀγανῶς οἷά τε νεβρὸν νεοθηλέα
γαλαθηνόν, ὅστ᾽ ἐν ὕλης κεροέσσης
ἀπολειφθεὶς ὑπὸ μητρὸς ἐπτοήθη.

8. *C.* I. 27, cf. III. 19. 9 sqq.—Anacreontis *fr.* 63.

Ἄγε δή, φέρ᾽ ἡμίν, ὦ παῖ,
κελέβην, ὅκως ἄμυστιν
προπίω, τὰ μὲν δέκ᾽ ἐγχέας
ὕδατος, τὰ πέντε δ᾽ οἴνου
κυάθους, ὡς ἀνυβριστί
ἀνὰ δηὗτε βασσαρήσω.

*   *

ἄγε δηὗτε μηκέθ᾽ οὕτω
πατάγῳ τε κἀλαλητῷ
Σκυθικὴν πόσιν παρ᾽ οἴνῳ
μελετῶμεν, ἀλλὰ καλοῖς
ὑποπίνοντες ἐν ὕμνοις.

9. *C.* I. 34. 12 sqq.—Archilochi *fr.* 56.

Τοῖς θεοῖς τίθει τὰ πάντα· πολλάκις μὲν ἐκ κακῶν
ἄνδρας ὀρθοῦσιν μελαίνῃ κειμένους ἐπὶ χθονί,
πολλάκις δ᾽ ἀνατρέπουσι καὶ μάλ᾽ εὖ βεβηκότας
ὑπτίους κλίνουσ᾽ . . .

10. *C.* I. 37.—Alcaei *fr.* 20.

Νῦν χρὴ μεθύσθην καί τινα πρὸς βίαν
πώνην, ἐπειδὴ κάτθανε Μύρσιλος.

11. *C.* II. 2.—Comici cuiusdam versus a Plutarcho (περὶ δυσωπίας 10) servatus:

Οὐκ ἔστ᾽ ἐν ἄντροις λευκός, ὦ ξέν᾽, ἄργυρος.

12. *C.* II. 7. 9 sqq.—Archilochi *fr.* 6.

Ἀσπίδι μὲν Σαΐων τις ἀγάλλεται, ἣν παρὰ θάμνῳ
ἔντος ἀμώμητον κάλλιπον οὐκ ἐθέλων·
αὐτὸς δ᾽ ἐξέφυγον θανάτου τέλος· ἀσπὶς ἐκείνη
ἐρρέτω· ἐξαῦτις κτήσομαι οὐ κακίω.

13. *C.* II. 18.—Bacchylidis *fr.* 28.

Οὐ βοῶν πάρεστι σώματ᾽, οὔτε χρυσός, οὔτε πορφύρεοι τάπητες,
ἀλλὰ θυμὸς εὐμενής,
Μοῦσά τε γλυκεῖα καὶ Βοιωτίοισιν ἐν σκύφοισιν οἶνος ἡδύς.

14. *C.* III. 2. 13.—Tyrtaei *fr.* 10.

Τεθνάμεναι γὰρ καλὸν ἐπὶ προμάχοισι πεσόντα
ἄνδρ' ἀγαθὸν περὶ ᾗ πατρίδι μαρνάμενον.

15. *C.* III. 2. 14.—Simonidis *fr.* 65.

Ὁ δ' αὖ θάνατος κίχε καὶ τὸν φυγόμαχον.

16. *C.* III. 2. 25.—Simonidis *fr.* 66.

Ἔστι καὶ σιγᾶς ἀκίνδυνον γέρας.

17. *C.* III. 4.—Alcmanis *fr.* 45.

Μῶσ' ἄγε, Καλλιόπα, θύγατερ Διός,
ἄρχ' ἐρατῶν ἐπέων . . .

18. *C.* III. 11. 9 sqq.—Anacreontis *fr.* 75.

Πῶλε Θρηκίη, τί δή με λοξὸν ὄμμασιν βλέπουσα
νηλεῶς φεύγεις, δοκέεις δέ μ' οὐδὲν εἰδέναι σοφόν;
       *   *
         *
νῦν δὲ λειμῶνάς τε βόσκεαι κοῦφά τε σκιρτῶσα παίζεις·
δεξιὸν γὰρ ἱπποσείρην οὐκ ἔχεις ἐπεμβάτην.

19. *C.* III. 12.—Alcaei *fr.* 59.

Ἔμε δείλαν, ἔμε πασᾶν κακοτάτων πεδέχοισαν.

20. *C.* IV. 3.—Hesiodi *theog.* 81 sqq.

Ὅντινα τιμήσωσι Διὸς κοῦραι μεγάλοιο
γεινόμενόν τε ἴδωσι διοτρεφέων βασιλήων,
τῷ μὲν ἐπὶ γλώσσῃ γλυκερὴν χείουσιν ἐέρσην,
τοῦ δ' ἔπε' ἐκ στόματος ῥεῖ μείλιχα . . .

21. *Epod.* 6. 13.—Archilochi *fr.* 94.

Πάτερ Λυκάμβα, ποῖον ἐφράσω τόδε;
   τίς σὰς παρήειρε φρένας;
ἧς τὸ πρὶν ἠρήρησθα· νῦν δὲ δὴ πολύς
   ἀστοῖσι φαίνεαι γέλως.

22. *Ep.* 13.—Anacreontis *fr.* 6.

       Μεὶς μὲν δὴ Ποσιδηϊών
       ἕστηκεν, νεφέλας δ' ὕδωρ
       βαρύνει, Δία τ' ἄγριοι
       χειμῶνες κατάγουσιν.

CARMINUM

LIBER PRIMUS.

I.

Maecenas atavis edite regibus,
o et praesidium et dulce decus meum:
sunt quos curriculo pulverem Olympicum
collegisse iuvat metaque fervidis
evitata rotis palmaque nobilis   5
terrarum dominos evehit ad deos:
hunc, si mobilium turba Quiritium
certat tergeminis tollere honoribus;
illum, si proprio condidit horreo
quicquid de Libycis verritur areis.   10

I. 5—10. With our punctuation, *hunc* of l. 7 is governed by *iuvat*
supplied from l. 4, though a distinct sentence *palmaque—deos* intervenes.
Many eminent scholars, from Pontanus (ob. 1639) to Dr Kennedy,
have preferred to put a full stop at *nobilis*, so that *terrarum* etc. begins
a new sentence: 'It raises to the gods this man if the crowd' etc.
This corrects the grammar and removes any doubt as to the meaning

gaudentem patrios findere sarculo
agros Attalicis condicionibus
numquam demoveas, ut trabe Cypria
Myrtoum pavidus nauta secet mare;
luctantem Icariis fluctibus Africum   15
mercator metuens otium et oppidi
laudat rura sui: mox reficit rates
quassas, indocilis pauperiem pati.
est qui nec veteris pocula Massici
nec partem solido demere de die   20
spernit, nunc viridi membra sub arbuto
stratus, nunc ad aquae lene caput sacrae.
multos castra iuvant et lituo tubae
permixtus sonitus bellaque matribus
detestata. manet sub Iove frigido   25
venator tenerae coniugis immemor,
seu visa est catulis cerva fidelibus,
seu rupit teretis Marsus aper plagas.
me doctarum hederae praemia frontium
dis miscent superis, me gelidum nemus   30
Nympharumque leves cum Satyris chori
secernunt populo, si neque tibias
Euterpe cohibet nec Polyhymnia
Lesboum refugit tendere barbiton.
quodsi me lyricis vatibus inseres,   35
sublimi feriam sidera vertice.

of *terrarum dominos*, but the construction and the choice of words
(*evehit—tollere*) and the sense (esp. *evehit illum si condidit* etc.) are very
awkward. In favour of the text, cf. IV. 2. 17 *quos Elea domum reducit
Palma caelestes*, where the idea of *palma—deos* is repeated, and observe
that, after the first two lines, we get a break at ll. 6, 10, 14, 18, 22.
These breaks mark the original stanzas, for the first two lines and the
last two were obviously added after the ode was finished.

II.

Iam satis terris nivis atque dirae
grandinis misit pater et rubente
dextera sacras iaculatus arces
    terruit urbem,

terruit gentis, grave ne rediret   5
saeculum Pyrrhae nova monstra questae,
omne cum Proteus pecus egit altos
    visere montis,

piscium et summa genus haesit ulmo,
nota quae sedes fuerat columbis,   10
et superiecto pavidae natarunt
    aequore dammae.

vidimus flavum Tiberim retortis
litore Etrusco violenter undis
ire deiectum monumenta regis   15
    templaque Vestae,

Iliae dum se nimium querenti
iactat ultorem, vagus et sinistra
labitur ripa Iove non probante u-
    xorius amnis.   20

audiet civis acuisse ferrum,
quo graves Persae melius perirent,
audiet pugnas vitio parentum
    rara iuventus.

quem vocet divum populus ruentis   25
imperi rebus? prece qua fatigent
virgines sanctae minus audientem
    carmina Vestam?

cui dabit partis scelus expiandi
Iuppiter? tandem venias precamur   30
nube candentis umeros amictus,
       augur Apollo;

sive tu mavis, Erycina ridens,
quam Iocus circum volat et Cupido;
sive neglectum genus et nepotes   35
       respicis, auctor

heu nimis longo satiate ludo,
quem iuvat clamor galeaeque leves,
acer et Mauri peditis cruentum
       vultus in hostem;   40

sive mutata iuvenem figura
ales in terris imitaris, almae
filius Maiae, patiens vocari
       Caesaris ultor:

serus in caelum redeas diuque   45
laetus intersis populo Quirini,
neve te nostris vitiis iniquum
       ocior aura

tollat; hic magnos potius triumphos,
hic ames dici pater atque princeps,   50
neu sinas Medos equitare inultos,
       te duce, Caesar.

II. 39. Bentley (following a suggestion of Tanaquil Faber, ob. 1672) read *Marsi peditis*, comparing II. 20. 18 and III. 5. 9, and denying *et pedites fuisse Mauros et fortes et cominus et galeatos in acie pugnavisse.* He supports his opinion, as usual, with great learning, but *Mauri peditis* may mean 'the Moor unhorsed' and Hor. may have been thinking of some well-known statue or picture. Cf. *Sat.* II. I. 15.

III.

Sic te diva potens Cypri,
    sic fratres Helenae, lucida sidera,
ventorumque regat pater
    obstrictis aliis praeter Iapyga,
navis, quae tibi creditum   5
    debes Vergilium, finibus Atticis
reddas incolumem precor
    et serves animae dimidium meae.
illi robur et aes triplex
    circa pectus erat, qui fragilem truci   10
commisit pelago ratem
    primus, nec timuit praecipitem Africum
decertantem Aquilonibus,
    nec tristis Hyadas, nec rabiem Noti,
quo non arbiter Hadriae   15
    maior, tollere seu ponere vult freta.
quem mortis timuit gradum,
    qui siccis oculis monstra natantia,
qui vidit mare turbidum et
    infamis scopulos Acroceraunia?   20
nequicquam deus abscidit
    prudens Oceano dissociabili
terras, si tamen impiae
    non tangenda rates transiliunt vada.
audax omnia perpeti   25
    gens humana ruit per vetitum nefas:
audax Iapeti genus
    ignem fraude mala gentibus intulit;
post ignem aetheria domo
    subductum macies et nova febrium   30

terris incubuit cohors,
    semotique prius tarda necessitas
leti corripuit gradum.
    expertus vacuum Daedalus aera
pennis non homini datis;   35
    perrupit Acheronta Herculeus labor.
nil mortalibus ardui est:
    caelum ipsum petimus stultitia, neque
per nostrum patimur scelus
    iracunda Iovem ponere fulmina.   40

IV.

Solvitur acris hiems grata vice veris et Favoni,
    trahuntque siccas machinae carinas,
ac neque iam stabulis gaudet pecus aut arator igni,
    nec prata canis albicant pruinis.
iam Cytherea choros ducit Venus imminente luna,   5
    iunctaeque Nymphis Gratiae decentes
alterno terram quatiunt pede, dum gravis Cyclopum
    Volcanus ardens visit officinas.
nunc decet aut viridi nitidum caput impedire myrto,
    aut flore, terrae quem ferunt solutae;   10
nunc et in umbrosis Fauno decet immolare lucis,
    seu poscat agna sive malit haedo.

IV. 8. The best MSS. have *visit*, but many have *urit*. In capitals
VISIT and VRIT are very similar, but there is no parallel for *urit* in
the sense required ('lights up'). A few inferior MSS. have *ussit* or
iussit, which, in Munro's opinion, arose from *vissit*, the Augustan
spelling of *visit*.

pallida mors aequo pulsat pede pauperum tabernas
    regumque turris. o beate Sesti,
vitae summa brevis spem nos vetat incohare longam. 15
    iam te premet nox fabulaeque manes
et domus exilis Plutonia: quo simul mearis,
    nec regna vini sortiere talis
nec tenerum Lycidan mirabere, quo calet iuventus
    nunc omnis et mox virgines tepebunt. 20

V.

    Quis multa gracilis te puer in rosa
    perfusus liquidis urget odoribus
       grato, Pyrrha, sub antro?
         cui flavam religas comam,

    simplex munditiis? heu quotiens fidem   5
    mutatosque deos flebit et aspera
       nigris aequora ventis
         emirabitur insolens,

    qui nunc te fruitur credulus aurea,
    qui semper vacuam, semper amabilem   10
       sperat, nescius aurae
         fallacis. miseri, quibus

    intemptata nites: me tabula sacer
    votiva paries indicat uvida
       suspendisse potenti   15
         vestimenta maris deo.

VI.

Scriberis Vario fortis et hostium
victor Maeonii carminis aliti,
quam rem cumque ferox navibus aut equis
    miles te duce gesserit.

nos, Agrippa, neque haec dicere, nec gravem   5
Pelidae stomachum cedere nescii,
nec cursus duplicis per mare Ulixei,
    nec saevam Pelopis domum

conamur, tenues grandia, dum pudor
imbellisque lyrae Musa potens vetat   10
laudes egregii Caesaris et tuas
    culpa deterere ingeni.

quis Martem tunica tectum adamantina
digne scripserit aut pulvere Troico
nigrum Merionem aut ope Palladis   15
    Tydiden superis parem?

nos convivia, nos proelia virginum
sectis in iuvenes unguibus acrium
cantamus vacui, sive quid urimur,
    non praeter solitum leves.   20

VI. 2. All MSS. have *alite*, but many editors (following Passeratius, ob. 1602) read *aliti*. No doubt, the dative of the agent is commonly used only with *compound* passive tenses. As Madvig says (on Cic. *De Fin.* I. iv. 11), Cicero could not have written *scribuntur nobis multa* but might have written *scripta sunt nobis*. But cf. *Epist.* I. 19. 3 *carmina quae scribuntur aquae potoribus*.

VII.

Laudabunt alii claram Rhodon aut Mytilenen
    aut Epheson bimarisve Corinthi
moenia vel Baccho Thebas vel Apolline Delphos
    insignis aut Thessala Tempe;
sunt quibus unum opus est intactae Palladis urbem 5
    carmine perpetuo celebrare et
undique decerptam fronti praeponere olivam;
    plurimus in Iunonis honorem
aptum dicet equis Argos ditisque Mycenas:
    me nec tam patiens Lacedaemon   10
nec tam Larisae percussit campus opimae
    quam domus Albuneae resonantis
et praeceps Anio ac Tiburni lucus et uda
    mobilibus pomaria rivis.
albus ut obscuro deterget nubila caelo   15
    saepe Notus neque parturit imbris
perpetuos, sic tu sapiens finire memento
    tristitiam vitaeque labores
molli, Plance, mero, seu te fulgentia signis
    castra tenent seu densa tenebit   20
Tiburis umbra tui. Teucer Salamina patremque
    cum fugeret, tamen uda Lyaeo
tempora populea fertur vinxisse corona,
    sic tristis affatus amicos:
'quo nos cumque feret melior fortuna parente,   25
    ibimus, o socii comitesque!
nil desperandum Teucro duce et auspice Teucro:
    certus enim promisit Apollo
ambiguam tellure nova Salamina futuram.
    o fortes peioraque passi   30
mecum saepe viri, nunc vino pellite curas:
    cras ingens iterabimus aequor.'

VIII.

Lydia, dic, per omnis
    te deos oro, Sybarin cur properes amando
perdere, cur apricum
    oderit campum, patiens pulveris atque solis,
cur neque militaris   5
    inter aequalis equitet, Gallica nec lupatis
temperet ora frenis?
    cur timet flavum Tiberim tangere? cur olivum
sanguine viperino
    cautius vitat neque iam livida gestat armis   10
bracchia, saepe disco,
    saepe trans finem iaculo nobilis expedito?
quid latet, ut marinae
    filium dicunt Thetidis sub lacrimosa Troiae
funera, ne virilis   15
    cultus in caedem et Lycias proriperet catervas?

IX.

Vides ut alta stet nive candidum
Soracte nec iam sustineant onus
    silvae laborantes geluque
        flumina constiterint acuto.

dissolve frigus ligna super foco   5
large reponens atque benignius
    deprome quadrimum Sabina,
        o Thaliarche, merum diota.

permitte divis cetera; qui simul
stravere ventos aequore fervido   10
    deproeliantis, nec cupressi
        nec veteres agitantur orni.

quid sit futurum cras, fuge quaerere, et
quem fors dierum cumque dabit, lucro
  appone, nec dulcis amores   15
    sperne puer neque tu choreas,

donec virenti canities abest
morosa. nunc et campus et areae
  lenesque sub noctem susurri
    composita repetantur hora,   20

nunc et latentis proditor intimo
gratus puellae risus ab angulo
  pignusque dereptum lacertis
    aut digito male pertinaci.

X.

Mercuri, facunde nepos Atlantis,
qui feros cultus hominum recentum
voce formasti catus et decorae
    more palaestrae,

te canam, magni Iovis et deorum   5
nuntium curvaeque lyrae parentem,
callidum quicquid placuit iocoso
    condere furto.

te, boves olim nisi reddidisses
per dolum amotas, puerum minaci   10
voce dum terret, viduus pharetra
    risit Apollo.

quin et Atridas duce te superbos
Ilio dives Priamus relicto
Thessalosque ignis et iniqua Troiae   15
    castra fefellit.

tu pias laetis animas reponis
sedibus virgaque levem coerces
aurea turbam, superis deorum
    gratus et imis.   20

XI.

Tu ne quaesieris (scire nefas) quem mihi, quem tibi
finem di dederint, Leuconoe, nec Babylonios
temptaris numeros. ut melius, quicquid erit, pati,
seu pluris hiemes seu tribuit Iuppiter ultimam,
quae nunc oppositis debilitat pumicibus mare   5
Tyrrhenum. sapias, vina liques et spatio brevi
spem longam reseces. dum loquimur, fugerit invida
aetas : carpe diem, quam minimum credula postero.

XII.

Quem virum aut heroa lyra vel acri
tibia sumis celebrare, Clio,
quem deum? cuius recinet iocosa
    nomen imago

aut in umbrosis Heliconis oris   5
aut super Pindo gelidove in Haemo?
unde vocalem temere insecutae
    Orphea silvae

arte materna rapidos morantem
fluminum lapsus celerisque ventos,   10
blandum et auritas fidibus canoris
    ducere quercus.

XI. 3—6. The punctuation is that of Bentley and Munro. Many
editors put a note of exclamation at *pati* and a comma at *Tyrrhenum.*

quid prius dicam solitis parentis
laudibus, qui res hominum ac deorum,
qui mare et terras variisque mundum   15
    temperat horis?

unde nil maius generatur ipso
nec viget quicquam simile aut secundum;
proximos illi tamen occupavit
    Pallas honores,   20

proeliis audax; neque te silebo,
Liber, et saevis inimica virgo
beluis, nec te, metuende certa
    Phoebe sagitta.

dicam et Alciden puerosque Ledae,   25
hunc equis, illum superare pugnis
nobilem; quorum simul alba nautis
    stella refulsit,

defluit saxis agitatus umor,
concidunt venti fugiuntque nubes,   30
et minax, quod sic voluere, ponto
    unda recumbit.

Romulum post hos prius, an quietum
Pompili regnum memorem, an superbos
Tarquini fasces, dubito, an Catonis   35
    nobile letum.

XII. 20, 21. The punctuation is Bentley's. Many editors put a
full stop at *honores* and refer *proeliis audax* to *Liber* (cf. II. 19. 21—28).
Prof. A. Palmer thinks that *proeliis audax* refers to Mars, who is not
otherwise named.

35—37. Cato seems incongruous among so many names from
ancient history. Hence Hamacher proposed *catenis nobilitatum
Regulum* and Prof. Housman *catenis (nobile!) laetum Reg.*

Regulum et Scauros animaeque magnae
prodigum Paulum superante Poeno
gratus insigni referam camena
    Fabriciumque.   40

hunc et incomptis Curium capillis
utilem bello tulit et Camillum
saeva paupertas et avitus apto
    cum lare fundus.

crescit occulto velut arbor aevo   45
fama Marcelli; micat inter omnis
Iulium sidus velut inter ignis
    luna minores.

gentis humanae pater atque custos,
orte Saturno, tibi cura magni   50
Caesaris fatis data: tu secundo
    Caesare regnes.

ille seu Parthos Latio imminentis
egerit iusto domitos triumpho
sive subiectos Orientis orae   55
    Seras et Indos,

te minor latum reget aequus orbem;
tu gravi curru quaties Olympum,
tu parum castis inimica mittes
    fulmina lucis.   60

---

46.   Many editors read *Marcellis*, 'the Marcelli,' a good suggestion
of Hofman Peerlkamp (ob. 1865).

XIII.

Cum tu, Lydia, Telephi
    cervicem roseam, cerea Telephi
laudas bracchia, vae meum
    fervens difficili bile tumet iecur.
tunc nec mens mihi nec color   5
    certa sede manent, umor et in genas
furtim labitur, arguens
    quam lentis penitus macerer ignibus.
uror, seu tibi candidos
    turparunt umeros immodicae mero   10
rixae, sive puer furens
    impressit memorem dente labris notam.
non, si me satis audias,
    speres perpetuum dulcia barbare
laedentem oscula, quae Venus   15
    quinta parte sui nectaris imbuit.
felices ter et amplius,
    quos irrupta tenet copula nec malis
divulsus querimoniis
    suprema citius solvet amor die.   20

XIV.

O navis, referent in mare te novi
fluctus! o quid agis? fortiter occupa
   portum! nonne vides ut
     nudum remigio latus

et malus celeri saucius Africo   5
antennaeque gemant ac sine funibus
   vix durare carinae
     possint imperiosius

aequor? non tibi sunt integra lintea,
non di, quos iterum pressa voces malo.   10
   quamvis Pontica pinus,
    silvae filia nobilis,

iactes et genus et nomen inutile,
nil pictis timidus navita puppibus
   fidit. tu nisi ventis   15
    debes ludibrium, cave.

nuper sollicitum quae mihi taedium,
nunc desiderium curaque non levis,
   interfusa nitentis
    vites aequora Cycladas.   20

XV.

Pastor cum traheret per freta navibus
Idaeis Helenen perfidus hospitam,
ingrato celeris obruit otio
   ventos ut caneret fera

Nereus fata: 'mala ducis avi domum,   5
quam multo repetet Graecia milite,
coniurata tuas rumpere nuptias
   et regnum Priami vetus.

heu heu, quantus equis, quantus adest viris
sudor! quanta moves funera Dardanae   10
genti! iam galeam Pallas et aegida
   currusque et rabiem parat.

nequicquam Veneris praesidio ferox
pectes caesariem grataque feminis
inbelli cithara carmina divides;   15
   nequicquam thalamo gravis

hastas et calami spicula Cnosii
vitabis strepitumque et celerem sequi
Aiacem : tamen, heu, serus adulteros
    crines pulvere collines. 20

non Laertiaden, exitium tuae
gentis, non Pylium Nestora respicis?
urgent impavidi te Salaminius
    Teucer, te Sthenelus sciens

pugnae, sive opus est imperitare equis, 25
non auriga piger. Merionen quoque
nosces. ecce furit te reperire atrox
    Tydides, melior patre :

quem tu, cervus uti vallis in altera
visum parte lupum graminis immemor, 30
sublimi fugies mollis anhelitu,
    non hoc pollicitus tuae.

iracunda diem proferet Ilio
matronisque Phrygum classis Achillei :
post certas hiemes uret Achaicus 35
    ignis Iliacas domos.'

XVI.

O matre pulchra filia pulchrior,
quem criminosis cumque voles modum
    pones iambis, sive flamma
      sive mari libet Hadriano.

xv. 36. The second syllable of the line ought to be long. It is
therefore probable that *Iliacas* is a gloss (suggested by *Ilio* l. 33)
for *Pergameas* or *barbaricas* or *Dardanias* or some such word
beginning with a consonant.

non Dindymene, non adytis quatit   5
mentem sacerdotum incola Pythius,
   non Liber aeque, non acuta
      si geminant Corybantes aera,

tristes ut irae, quas neque Noricus
deterret ensis nec mare naufragum   10
   nec saevus ignis nec tremendo
      Iuppiter ipse ruens tumultu.

fertur Prometheus addere principi
limo coactus particulam undique
   desectam et insani leonis   15
      vim stomacho apposuisse nostro.

irae Thyesten exitio gravi
stravere et altis urbibus ultimae
   stetere causae, cur perirent
      funditus imprimeretque muris   20

hostile aratrum exercitus insolens.
compesce mentem ! me quoque pectoris
   temptavit in dulci iuventa
      fervor et in celeris iambos

misit furentem : nunc ego mitibus   25
mutare quaero tristia, dum mihi
   fias recantatis amica
      opprobriis animumque reddas.

XVI. 8. The MSS. with one doubtful exception have *sic geminant.*
Bentley's reading *si* has been largely adopted by editors.

XVII.

Velox amoenum saepe Lucretilem
mutat Lycaeo Faunus et igneam
    defendit aestatem capellis
        usque meis pluviosque ventos.

impune tutum per nemus arbutos   5
quaerunt latentis et thyma deviae
    olentis uxores mariti,
        nec viridis metuunt colubras

nec Martialis haediliae lupos,
utcumque dulci, Tyndari, fistula   10
    valles et Usticae cubantis
        levia personuere saxa.

di me tuentur, dis pietas mea
et Musa cordi est. hinc tibi copia
    manabit ad plenum benigno   15
        ruris honorum opulenta cornu.

hic in reducta valle Caniculae
vitabis aestus et fide Teia
    dices laborantis in uno
        Penelopen vitreamque Circen.   20

hic innocentis pocula Lesbii
duces sub umbra, nec Semeleius
    cum Marte confundet Thyoneus
        proelia, nec metues protervum

suspecta Cyrum, ne male dispari   25
incontinentis iniciat manus
    et scindat haerentem coronam
        crinibus immeritamque vestem.

2—2

XVIII.

Nullam, Vare, sacra vite prius severis arborem
circa mite solum Tiburis et moenia Catili:
siccis omnia nam dura deus proposuit, neque
mordaces aliter diffugiunt sollicitudines.
quis post vina gravem militiam aut pauperiem crepat? 5
quis non te potius, Bacche pater, teque, decens Venus?
ac nequis modici transiliat munera Liberi,
Centaurea monet cum Lapithis rixa super mero
debellata, monet Sithoniis non levis Euhius,
cum fas atque nefas exiguo fine libidinum 10
discernunt avidi. non ego te, candide Bassareu,
invitum quatiam nec variis obsita frondibus
sub divum rapiam. saeva tene cum Berecyntio
cornu tympana, quae subsequitur caecus amor sui
et tollens vacuum plus nimio gloria verticem 15
arcanique fides prodiga, perlucidior vitro.

XIX.

Mater saeva Cupidinum
    Thebanaeque iubet me Semelae puer
et lasciva Licentia
    finitis animum reddere amoribus.
urit me Glycerae nitor 5
    splendentis Pario marmore purius,
urit grata protervitas
    et vultus nimium lubricus aspici.
in me tota ruens Venus
    Cyprum deseruit, nec patitur Scythas 10
et versis animosum equis
    Parthum dicere nec quae nihil attinent.

hic vivum mihi caespitem, hic
    verbenas, pueri, ponite turaque
bimi cum patera meri :   15
    mactata veniet lenior hostia.

XX.

Vile potabis modicis Sabinum
cantharis, Graeca quod ego ipse testa
conditum levi, datus in theatro
    cum tibi plausus,

care Maecenas eques, ut paterni   5
fluminis ripae simul et iocosa
redderet laudes tibi Vaticani
    montis imago.

Caecubum et prelo domitam Caleno
tu †bibes uvam : mea nec Falernae   10
temperant vites neque Formiani
    pocula colles.

xx. 10. *Tu bibes* is the reading of the MSS. but it can hardly be
right. Hor. is not likely to have written *potabis* in l. 1 meaning 'you
will drink at my house' and *bibes* in l. 10 meaning 'you can drink at
your own house.' Porphyrion (on *Sat.* II. 2. 48) quotes the words as
Tum bibes and many edd. print this, rendering it 'Afterwards you shall
drink Caecuban and Calenian.' But these wines were the best and
most expensive, whereas the point of the ode is that Hor. was poor
(cf. *vile* and *modicis* in l. 1). Besides, *tu* is supported by the emphatic
mea which follows. Many conjectures have been made, but the true
reading is doubtless *tu iubes*, 'you order,' for which cp. *Ep.* II. 2. 63
renuis tu quod iubet alter.

XXI.

Dianam tenerae dicite virgines,
intonsum, pueri, dicite Cynthium
   Latonamque supremo
     dilectam penitus Iovi.

vos laetam fluviis et nemorum coma,   5
quaecumque aut gelido prominet Algido,
   nigris aut Erymanthi
     silvis aut viridis Cragi.

vos Tempe totidem tollite laudibus
natalemque, mares, Delon Apollinis   10
   insignemque pharetra
     fraternaque umerum lyra.

hic bellum lacrimosum, hic miseram famem
pestemque a populo et principe Caesare in
   Persas atque Britannos   15
     vestra motus aget prece.

XXII.

   Integer vitae scelerisque purus
   non eget Mauris iaculis neque arcu
   nec venenatis gravida sagittis,
     Fusce, pharetra,

   sive per Syrtis iter aestuosas   5
   sive facturus per inhospitalem
   Caucasum vel quae loca fabulosus
     lambit Hydaspes.

namque me silva lupus in Sabina,
dum meam canto Lalagen et ultra　　10
terminum curis vagor expeditis,
　　fugit inermem,

quale portentum neque militaris
Daunias latis alit aesculetis
nec Iubae tellus generat, leonum　　15
　　arida nutrix.

pone me pigris ubi nulla campis
arbor aestiva recreatur aura,
quod latus mundi nebulae malusque
　　Iuppiter urget;　　20

pone sub curru nimium propinqui
solis, in terra domibus negata:
dulce ridentem Lalagen amabo,
　　dulce loquentem.

XXIII.

Vitas hinnuleo me similis, Chloe,
quaerenti pavidam montibus aviis
　　matrem non sine vano
　　aurarum et siluae metu.

nam seu mobilibus vepris inhorruit　　5
ad ventum foliis, seu virides rubum
　　dimovere lacertae,
　　et corde et genibus tremit.

XXIII. 5, 6. The text is Bentley's, founded on earlier conjectures.
The MSS. have *veris inhorruit adventus* and many edd. contend that
this is good Latin and a pretty expression. It may be that 'the
approach of spring bristles with (*or* on) the leaves' is a good hypallage
for 'the leaves bristle with the approach of the spring.' But here the

atqui non ego te tigris ut aspera
Gaetulusve leo frangere persequor: 10
   tandem desine matrem
      tempestiva sequi viro.

XXIV.

Quis desiderio sit pudor aut modus
tam cari capitis? praecipe lugubris
cantus, Melpomene, cui liquidam pater
   vocem cum cithara dedit.

ergo Quintilium perpetuus sopor   5
urget? cui Pudor et Iustitiae soror,
incorrupta Fides, nudaque Veritas
   quando ullum inveniet parem?

multis ille bonis flebilis occidit,
nulli flebilior quam tibi, Vergili.   10
tu frustra pius heu non ita creditum
   poscis Quintilium deos.

quid, si Threicio blandius Orpheo
auditam moderere arboribus fidem?
num vanae redeat sanguis imagini,   15
   quam virga semel horrida,

non lenis precibus fata recludere,
nigro compulerit Mercurius gregi?
durum: sed levius fit patientia
   quicquid corrigere est nefas.   20

leaves bristle so suddenly as to startle the fawn, and this effect cannot
reasonably be assigned to the approach of spring. Moreover, 'the
approach of spring' and 'a lizard in the bush' are absurd alternatives.
The reading *ad ventum* is confirmed too by *aurarum* of l. 4.

    XXIV. 13.   Many edd. read *quod si*, but all the best MSS. have *quid
si*: cf. *Sat.* II. 3. 159 and 219: 7. 42: *Epist.* I. 16. 8: 19. 12.

XXV.

Parcius iunctas quatiunt fenestras
iactibus crebris iuvenes protervi
nec tibi somnos adimunt, amatque
    ianua limen,

quae prius multum facilis movebat   5
cardines. audis minus et minus iam:
'me tuo longas pereunte noctes,
    Lydia, dormis?'

invicem moechos anus arrogantis
flebis in solo levis angiportu,   10
Thracio bacchante magis sub inter-
    lunia vento,

cum tibi flagrans amor et libido,
quae solet matres furiare equorum,
saeviet circa iecur ulcerosum,   15
    non sine questu,

laeta quod pubes hedera virenti
gaudeat pulla magis atque myrto,
aridas frondes hiemis sodali
    dedicet Euro.   20

XXV. 20. The reading *Euro* is due to the editor of the Aldine
edition of 1501. The MSS. and scholiasts have *Hebro*. The words
were certainly liable to confusion and the wind Eurus is more likely
than the river Hebrus to be called *hiemis sodalis* (cf. I. 28. 21, 22 and
IV. 12. 1, 2). Vergil, *Georg.* II. 339, has *hibernis flatibus Euri*. The
same emendation, *Eurum* for *Hebrum*, has been proposed in *Aeneid*
I. 317.

XXVI.

Musis amicus tristitiam et metus
tradam protervis in mare Creticum
    portare ventis, quis sub Arcto
      rex gelidae metuatur orae,

quid Tiridaten terreat, unice   5
securus. o quae fontibus integris
    gaudes, apricos necte flores,
      necte meo Lamiae coronam,

Pimplei dulcis. nil sine te mei
prosunt honores : hunc fidibus novis,   10
    hunc Lesbio sacrare plectro
      teque tuasque decet sorores.

XXVII.

Natis in usum laetitiae scyphis
pugnare Thracum est : tollite barbarum
    morem verecundumque Bacchum
      sanguineis prohibete rixis.

vino et lucernis Medus acinaces   5
immane quantum discrepat : impium
    lenite clamorem, sodales,
      et cubito remanete presso.

vultis severi me quoque sumere
partem Falerni? dicat Opuntiae   10
    frater Megyllae, quo beatus
      vulnere, qua pereat sagitta.

XXVI. 9. *Pimplei* is Bentley's reading. The MSS. have *Piplea*.

cessat voluntas ? non alia bibam
mercede. quae te cumque domat Venus,
   non erubescendis adurit   15
      ignibus ingenuoque semper

amore peccas. quicquid habes, age
depone tutis auribus. a miser,
   quanta laborabas Charybdi,
      digne puer meliore flamma !   20

quae saga, quis te solvere Thessalis
magus venenis, quis poterit deus ?
   vix illigatum te triformi
      Pegasus expediet Chimaera.

XXVIII.

Te maris et terrae numeroque carentis harenae
   mensorem cohibent, Archyta,
pulveris exigui prope litus parva Matinum
   munera, nec quicquam tibi prodest
aerias temptasse domos animoque rotundum   5
   percurrisse polum morituro.
occidit et Pelopis genitor, conviva deorum,
   Tithonusque remotus in auras
et Iovis arcanis Minos admissus, habentque
   Tartara Panthoiden iterum Orco   10
demissum, quamvis clipeo Troiana refixo
   tempora testatus nihil ultra
nervos atque cutem morti concesserat atrae,
   iudice te non sordidus auctor
naturae verique. sed omnis una manet nox   15
   et calcanda semel via leti.

dant alios Furiae torvo spectacula Marti,
    exitio est avidum mare nautis;
mixta senum ac iuvenum densentur funera, nullum
    saeva caput Proserpina fugit.   20
me quoque devexi rapidus comes Orionis
    Illyricis Notus obruit undis.
at tu, nauta, vagae ne parce malignus harenae
    ossibus et capiti inhumato
particulam dare: sic, quodcumque minabitur Eurus 25
    fluctibus Hesperiis, Venusinae
plectantur silvae te sospite, multaque merces,
    unde potest, tibi defluat aequo
ab Iove Neptunoque sacri custode Tarenti.
    neglegis immeritis nocituram   30
postmodo te natis fraudem committere? forset
    debita iura vicesque superbae
te maneant ipsum: precibus non linquar inultis,
    teque piacula nulla resolvent.
quamquam festinas, non est mora longa: licebit 35
    iniecto ter pulvere curras.

XXIX.

Icci, beatis nunc Arabum invides
gazis et acrem militiam paras
    non ante devictis Sabaeae
      regibus horribilique Medo

nectis catenas? quae tibi virginum   5
sponso necato barbara serviet?
    puer quis ex aula capillis
      ad cyathum statuetur unctis,

doctus sagittas tendere Sericas
arcu paterno? quis neget arduis   10
   pronos relabi posse rivos
     montibus et Tiberim reverti,

cum tu coemptos undique nobilis
libros Panaeti, Socraticam et domum
   mutare loricis Hiberis,   15
     pollicitus meliora, tendis?

XXX.

O Venus regina Cnidi Paphique,
sperne dilectam Cypron et vocantis
   ture te multo Glycerae decoram
     transfer in aedem.

fervidus tecum puer et solutis   5
Gratiae zonis properentque Nymphae
et parum comis sine te Iuventas
     Mercuriusque.

XXXI.

Quid dedicatum poscit Apollinem
vates? quid orat de patera novum
   fundens liquorem? non opimae
     Sardiniae segetes feraces,

non aestuosae grata Calabriae   5
armenta, non aurum aut ebur Indicum,
   non rura, quae Liris quieta
     mordet aqua taciturnus amnis.

premant Calena falce quibus dedit
Fortuna vitem, dives ut aureis   10
   mercator exsiccet culullis
     vina Syra reparata merce,

dis carus ipsis, quippe ter et quater
anno revisens aequor Atlanticum
   impune : me pascunt olivae,   15
     me cichorea levesque malvae.

frui paratis et valido mihi,
Latoe, dones et, precor, integra
   cum mente nec turpem senectam
     degere nec cithara carentem.   20

XXXII.

Poscimur. siquid vacui sub umbra
lusimus tecum, quod et hunc in annum
vivat et pluris, age dic Latinum,
    barbite, carmen,

Lesbio primum modulate civi,   5
qui ferox bello tamen inter arma,
sive iactatam religarat udo
    litore navem,

XXXI. 13—16. This stanza is perhaps an interpolation. A
merchant would not get *Syra merx* by trading to the Atlantic, and the
details of Hor.'s diet are both abrupt and unnecessary.

18. The MSS. have *at precor*. Lambinus (ob. 1572) read *et*,
Bentley *ac*.

XXXII. 1. Many of the best MSS. have *poscimus:* but *poscimur* is
better suited to the emphatic position and is supported by Ovid,
Met. II. 144 and V. 333.

Liberum et Musas Veneremque et illi
semper haerentem puerum canebat   10
et Lycum nigris oculis nigroque
    crine decorum.

o decus Phoebi et dapibus supremi
grata testudo Iovis, o laborum
dulce lenimen, mihi cumque salve   15
    rite vocanti !

XXXIII.

Albi, ne doleas plus nimio memor
immitis Glycerae, neu miserabilis
decantes elegos, cur tibi iunior
    laesa praeniteat fide.

insignem tenui fronte Lycorida   5
Cyri torret amor, Cyrus in asperam
declinat Pholoen : sed prius Apulis
    iungentur capreae lupis,

quam turpi Pholoe peccet adultero.
sic visum Veneri, cui placet imparis   10
formas atque animos sub iuga aenea
    saevo mittere cum ioco.

15. The reading of all MSS., *mihi cumque salve*, has provoked a host of conjectures. Certainly *cumque* is not elsewhere found by itself and, again, though *salve mihi* is a common expression, *mihi* is here usually a mere ethical dative, incapable of supporting an epithet, let alone so strong a limitation as *rite vocanti*. The text however is better than the emendations (*medicumque, mihi tu usque, melicumque, metuumque, mihi iunge* etc.).

ipsum me melior cum peteret Venus,
grata detinuit compede Myrtale
libertina, fretis acrior Hadriae   15
    curvantis Calabros sinus.

XXXIV.

Parcus deorum cultor et infrequens,
insanientis dum sapientiae
    consultus erro, nunc retrorsum
        vela dare atque iterare cursus

cogor relictos : namque Diespiter,   5
igni corusco nubila dividens
    plerumque, per purum tonantis
        egit equos volucremque currum,

quo bruta tellus et vaga flumina,
quo Styx et invisi horrida Taenari   10
    sedes Atlanteusque finis
        concutitur.   valet ima summis

mutare et insignem attenuat deus,
obscura promens : hinc apicem rapax
    Fortuna cum stridore acuto   15
        sustulit, hic posuisse gaudet.

XXXV.

O diva, gratum quae regis Antium,
praesens vel imo tollere de gradu
    mortale corpus vel superbos
        vertere funeribus triumphos :

te pauper ambit sollicita prece   5
ruris colonus, te dominam aequoris
    quicumque Bithyna lacessit
     Carpathium pelagus carina;

te Dacus asper, te profugi Scythae
urbesque gentesque et Latium ferox   10
    regumque matres barbarorum et
     purpurei metuunt tyranni,

iniurioso ne pede proruas
stantem columnam, neu populus frequens
    ad arma cessantis, ad arma   15
     concitet imperiumque frangat:

te semper anteit saeva Necessitas,
clavos trabalis et cuneos manu
    gestans aena, nec severus
     uncus abest liquidumque plumbum: 20

te Spes et albo rara Fides colit
velata panno nec comitem abnegat,
    utcumque mutata potentis
     veste domos inimica linquis.

at vulgus infidum et meretrix retro   25
periura cedit, diffugiunt cadis
    cum faece siccatis amici,
     ferre iugum pariter dolosi.

serves iturum Caesarem in ultimos
orbis Britannos et iuvenum recens   30
    examen Eois timendum
     partibus Oceanoque rubro.

xxxv. 17. The reading *serva Necessitas* is somewhat more strongly supported by MSS. than *saeva Nec.* The words are elsewhere confused (as Bentley points out) and *saeva* seems the more appropriate.

eheu, cicatricum et sceleris pudet
fratrumque. quid nos dura refugimus
   aetas? quid intactum nefasti   35
      liquimus? unde manum iuventus

metu deorum continuit? quibus
pepercit aris? o utinam nova
   incude diffingas retunsum in
      Massagetas Arabasque ferrum.   40

XXXVI.

Et ture et fidibus iuvat
   placare et vituli sanguine debito
custodes Numidae deos,
   qui nunc Hesperia sospes ab ultima
caris multa sodalibus,   5
   nulli plura tamen dividit oscula
quam dulci Lamiae, memor
   actae non alio rege puertiae
mutataeque simul togae.
   Cressa ne careat pulchra dies nota,   10
neu promptae modus amphorae
   neu morem in Salium sit requies pedum,
neu multi Damalis meri
   Bassum Threicia vincat amystide,
neu desint epulis rosae   15
   neu vivax apium neu breve lilium.
omnes in Damalin putris
   deponent oculos, nec Damalis novo
divelletur adultero,
   lascivis hederis ambitiosior.   20

XXXVII.

Nunc est bibendum, nunc pede libero
pulsanda tellus; nunc Saliaribus
   ornare pulvinar deorum
    tempus erat dapibus, sodales.

antehac nefas depromere Caecubum   5
cellis avitis, dum Capitolio
   regina dementis ruinas
    funus et imperio parabat

contaminato cum grege turpium
morbo virorum, quidlibet impotens   10
   sperare fortunaque dulci
    ebria. sed minuit furorem

vix una sospes navis ab ignibus,
mentemque lymphatam Mareotico
   redegit in veros timores   15
    Caesar, ab Italia volantem

remis adurgens, accipiter velut
mollis columbas aut leporem citus
   venator in campis nivalis
    Haemoniae, daret ut catenis   20

fatale monstrum. quae generosius
perire quaerens nec muliebriter
   expavit ensem nec latentis
    classe cita reparavit oras;

XXXVII. 24. Almost all MSS. have *reparavit*. One (*R*, a pretty
good one) is said to have *repetivit*, but several edd. who used this MS.
do not notice this reading. Many emendations have been proposed:
e.g. *penetravit, remeavit, properavit, repedavit, peraravit, ire paravit*
etc.

ausa et iacentem visere regiam   25
vultu sereno fortis et asperas
   tractare serpentes, ut atrum
     corpore combiberet venenum,

deliberata morte ferocior,
saevis Liburnis scilicet invidens   30
   privata deduci superbo
     non humilis mulier triumpho.

XXXVIII.

Persicos odi, puer, apparatus,
displicent nexae philyra coronae:
mitte sectari, rosa quo locorum
   sera moretur.

simplici myrto nihil allabores   5
sedulus, curo: neque te ministrum
dedecet myrtus neque me sub arta
   vite bibentem.

NOTES.

BOOK I.

Ode I.

To C. Cilnius Maecenas, Horace's patron and benefactor. He was born April 13th (*Carm.* IV. II. 14–16), about B.C. 69, and died B.C. 8, a few months before Horace himself. He was of Etruscan descent (*Carm.* III. 29. 1) and of equestrian rank (*Carm.* I. 20. 5). He never held any of the great republican offices in Rome, but was largely concerned in the politics of Octavian's early career and was more than once, during O.'s absence, entrusted with the government of Rome and Italy (Tac. *Ann.* VI. 11). Horace was introduced to him in B.C. 39 and received from him the most generous treatment. (See *Introd.* pp. xii–xv.) No less than sixteen of Horace's compositions are addressed to him.

Scheme. Different men have different pursuits. This one loves horse-racing: that politics: another commerce or agriculture or war or hunting. My choice is poesy and my ambition is to be counted among the lyrists.

Metre. The First Asclepiad (*Introd.* p. xxx).

1. **atavis...regibus**, 'royal ancestors.' The Cilnii came originally from Arretium in Etruria (Livy X. 3), and it would seem that Maecenas cherished a tradition that they were of royal rank. He is addressed as *Tyrrhena regum progenies* in *C.* III. 29. 1, and by Propertius (III. 9. 1) as *eques Etrusco de sanguine regum*.

For the ablative, cf. *orte Saturno*, I. 12. 50 : and for the apposition *atavis...regibus* cf. *fabulae manes*, I. 4. 16.

The Latin order of ascent was *pater, avus, proavus, abavus, atavus, tritavus*.

2. **o et.** For the hiatus, cf. *o utinam*, I. 35. 38 and IV. 5. 37.

For the address, cf. II. 17. 4 *Maecenas mearum grande decus columenque rerum:* and Vergil, *Georg.* II. 40, *o decus, o famae merito pars maxima nostrae, Maecenas.*

3, 4. **sunt quos...iuvat.** *sunt qui* (or *est qui*) is usually followed by the consecutive subj., the sense being 'there are men such that...' (cf. *dignus* *qui* with subj.): but the indic. may follow where *sunt qui* or *est qui* is merely equivalent to *nonnulli* or *non nemo*. It often happens however (e.g. *Epist.* II. 2. 182 *sunt qui non habeant, est qui non curat habere*) that the indic. is used where *sunt qui* (or *est qui*) refers to a definite group (or person): whereas the subj. is used where the reference is to a vague ill-defined group (or person). The indic. is used below *v.* 19 and in I. 7. 5.

curriculo probably means 'with the chariot' (as in Ov. *Trist.* IV. 8. 36 *curriculo gravis est facta ruina mco*), not 'on the race-course.' With the latter meaning we should expect *Olympico* instead of *Olympicum*.

pulverem...collegisse, 'to have raised a cloud of dust,' cf. *collectus turbine pulvis*, *Sat.* I. 4. 31. For the perf. cf. *gaudet pepulisse fossor*, III. 18. 15 and see Roby's *Latin Grammar* § 1371. The present infin. is used in IV. 1. 31.

Olympicum. The reference is to the great Olympian games held at Pisa in Elis, in honour of Olympian Zeus. The epithet is hardly natural in a Roman writer, but Horace, as an avowed imitator of Greek poets, very often adopts from them familiar epithets: e.g. *Cypria, Myrtoum, Icariis* below ll. 13–15.

4. meta, 'the turning-post,' with which it was fatal to collide. In Sophocles' *Electra*, 720–748, there is a description of a chariot-race in which Orestes took part. It is told how, in the earlier rounds, he artfully took the turn so close as to shave the post, but in the last round he struck it and was upset.

5. evitata. The preposition has some suggestion of an ejaculation from the excited spectators, cf. *emirabitur* in I. 5. 6.

palma nobilis, 'the glorious palm.' The prize at Olympian games was a crown of wild olives, but a palm-branch also was given to the victor at these and all the other great games.

6. terrarum dominos, in apposition with *deos*: as in Ovid, *Epp. ex Ponto* I. 9. 36 *terrarum dominos quam colis ipse deos*. Some scholars prefer to take *dominos* as part of the accus. after *evehit* ('raises them to heaven, very lords of the world,' Wickham). In Horace's way of reading the line (which we do not know, see *Introd.* p. xxvi) the meaning must have been plain, and the quotation from Ovid seems the best clue to it. The sentiment is repeated IV. 2. 17 *quos Elea domum reducit palma caelestes*. On the punctuation, see Critical Note.

7. hunc is governed by *iuvat* in l. 4, the intervening sentence *palmaque...deos* being a picturesque parenthesis, such as we often find in similes, e.g. IV. 4. 1–16.

mobilium turba Q. Cf. Tac. *Hist.* v. 8 (*reges*) *mobilitate vulgi expulsi*. In Horace's time the forms of popular election were still maintained and statutes were passed to prevent bribery and rioting at the comitia, but the magistrates were mere nominees of Augustus. See Pelham's *Roman History*, pp. 388–391.

8. tergeminis honoribus (instr. abl.) seems to refer to the regular *cursus honorum* of quaestor, praetor and consul.

9. **proprio** = *suo proprio.* The possessive pronoun is rarely omitted in Cicero.

horreo, cf. III. 16. 26 *si quicquid arat impiger Appulus Occultare meis dicerer horreis.*

10. **Libycis.** Corn was at this time imported chiefly from the province of Africa (in the neighbourhood of Tunis). Egypt afterwards became the chief corn-mart. Cf. *fertilis Africa,* III. 16. 31.

verritur, 'is swept' after threshing.

11. **gaudentem,** 'him who delights to break the clods of his ancestral fields,' i.e. the farmer who tills with his own hands.

12. **Attalicis condicionibus,** 'with offers such as Attalus might have made'; i.e. *regiis opibus.* Attalus III., king of Pergamus, bequeathed his kingdom to Rome B.C. 133. It was organized as the province of Asia and was the richest of the Roman possessions.

13. **Cypria.** Ammianus Marcellinus, XIV. 8. 14, says that every part of a ship, from keel to truck, could be produced in Cyprus. For the epithets in this and following lines, cf. note supra on *Olympicum,* v. 3.

ut is consecutive, not final. If it were final, we should require *impavidus nauta* in 14.

14. **Myrtoum mare** was the western part of the Aegean, so named from the small island Myrto, south of Euboea.

15. **Icariis...fluctibus,** dat.: cf. Epod. 2. 20 *certantem et uvam purpurae.*

The Icarian sea is the eastern part of the Aegean, so named from Icaria, a small island west of Samos.

Africum, the south-west wind. Its violence is again alluded to in I. 3. 12.

16. **metuens,** 'when he fears': for he soon forgets his terror. Cf. II. 16. 1-2 *otium divos rogat in potenti prensus Aegaeo.*

otium et rura, 'peaceful life and landscapes.'

18. **indocilis...pati.** For the infin. see *Introd.* p. xxiii.

pauperiem, not poverty (*egestas*), but 'modest means.' Kiessling quotes from Seneca, *Epp.* LXXXVII. 40, *non video quid aliud sit paupertas quam parvi possessio.*

19. **Massici,** a celebrated wine grown on the Campanian hills near Sinuessa. It is praised in II. 7. 21 and III. 21. 6.

There is no special appropriateness in *Massic* wine, any more than there was in the *Cyprian* bark or *Myrtoan* sea or *Icarian* waves of ll. 13-15. The epithets are (as we say nowadays) 'realistic,' i.e. they create an impression that the poet has particular scenes vividly in mind. A very fine example of the device is Milton's

'Thick as autumnal leaves that strew the brooks
In Vallombrosa, where the Etrurian shades
High over-arched embower.'   *Par. Lost,* I. 302.

20. nec...die, 'to break into the working day' (cf. II. 7. 7 *diem mero fregi*). *Solidus dies* was that part of the day which should be given to uninterrupted work: cf. Seneca, *Ep.* LXXXIII., *hodiernus dies solidus est: nemo ex illo mihi quidquam eripuit.* To drink wine before dinner-time (the ninth or tenth hour) was dissipated behaviour. See Mayor's note on Juvenal I. 49. In German, a loafing lazy fellow is called a *tagedieb* or 'day-thief.'

21. arbuto. The arbutus, or strawberry-tree, forms a large bush, often 20 feet high.

22. lene caput, 'a softly-murmuring spring.'

sacrae. All springs were sacred, as being the haunts of water-nymphs. Shrines (*sacella*) were often placed beside them.

23. lituo. The *lituus* was a horn bent at the end. It was used as a bugle by cavalry.

tubae. The *tuba* was a straight horn, used by infantry. The *lituus* was shriller than the *tuba*.

25. detestata, passive, 'abhorred.' Cf. *abominatus.*

Iove, 'the sky.' Cf. Epod. XIII. 2 *nivesque deducunt Iovem. sub divo* is similarly used for 'in the open air' in II. 3. 23, III. 11. 5. In I. 22. 20 *malus Iuppiter* means 'a bad climate.'

28. teretes is used (in a complimentary sense) of ankles in II. 4. 21 and of a boy in *Epod.* XI. 28. It is used by other writers of such things as a thread, a wand and a pebble. It seems to combine the qualities of *smooth, round* and *slim.* Here it obviously refers to the twine of which the nets are made and probably means 'thin.' The nets are set for roe-deer, but the boar bursts through them. Some scholars think it means 'tightly-twisted' and therefore 'strong.'

Marsus aper. The Marsi lived in Latium near *lacus Fucinus.* For boar-hunting in Italy, cf. III. 12. 11 and *Epist.* I. 18. 55.

29. doctarum, not 'learned,' but 'cultured.' Like the Greek σοφός, *doctus* is especially applied to poets, as Tibullus I. 4. 61 *Pieridas, pueri, doctos et amate poetas.*

hederae. The ivy was sacred to Bacchus, the god of inspiration. Cf. Verg. *Ecl.* VII. 28 *pastores hedera crescentem ornate poetam.*

gelidum nemus, not any real place, but the fancied grove, haunted by the *di superi* and Muses and nymphs.

32–34. tibias, double pipes, used as an accompaniment to *choral* odes.

barbiton, a large seven-stringed lyre, such as Alcaeus (see I. 32. 5) and other Lesbian poets used as an accompaniment to *songs.*

The *tibiae* and *barbitos*, therefore, are equivalent to lyric poetry of both kinds (cf. *Introd.* p. xviii). The former are here ascribed to Euterpe, the latter to Polyhymnia, but both are attributed by Hor. to Clio (invoked in I. 12. 1–2) and to Calliope (invoked in III. 4. 1–4). In IV. 3 Hor. says that he owes his inspiration to Melpomene. Evidently, he did not know or heed the division of functions assigned to the several Muses.

NOTES. 41

tendere, 'to tune' by tightening the strings, or 'to string' (like *tendit arcum* in II. 10. 19).

35. **inseres.** The subject is Maecenas. 'If you, Maecenas (when you have read these poems), add me to the choir of lyric poets.' For the verb, cf. II. 5. 21 and III. 25. 6.

lyricis vatibus. The allusion is to the Greek canon of nine lyrists, viz. Pindar, Alcaeus, Sappho, Stesichorus, Ibycus, Bacchylides, Simonides, Alcman, Anacreon.

Ode II.

The ode is addressed to Caesar (Octavianus, not yet Augustus), but the date is uncertain. It was written, obviously, in winter after snowstorms and floods (vv. 1–20), at a time when Caesar was in Rome (v. 46) and when there seemed no reason why he should go away. There were two occasions when he was received in Rome with special exultation: the first, in Nov., B.C. 36, after conquering S. Pompeius: the second, in July, B.C. 29, after conquering Antony and Cleopatra. In August of the latter year he celebrated a splendid triumph, to which v. 49 of the ode may refer. Moreover, in the course of B.C. 28 he gave out that he had completed his mission of avenging his uncle Julius and meant to surrender all his powers to the senate on Jan. 1st, B.C. 27. The announcement would naturally cause such alarm as is expressed in this ode. It might therefore have been written in Decr. B.C. 28. Dion Cassius (LIII. 20) expressly mentions a great flood in Rome about Jan., B.C. 27, but by that time the political alarm was over, for the senate had given to Octavian imperial powers. Nevertheless, the winter of B.C. 28–27 seems, on the whole, the most probable date for the composition of the ode. A very fine passage, of much the same tenour as this ode, occurs at the end of Vergil's First Georgic, which seems to have been written in B.C. 32, a short time before the battle of Actium.

Scheme. We are sick of horrors. Storms and floods and civil strife have brought us near to ruin. What god will arise to save us? Is it thou, Mercury, disguised as Caesar? Ah, stay yet awhile and bring us peace for many a day.

Metre. Sapphic (*Introd.* p. xxix).

1. **terris**, dat. as in I. 12. 59 *mittes fulmina lucis.*

dirae, a specially appropriate epithet, since the word was supposed to be derived from *deorum ira.* Here it qualifies both *nivis* and *grandinis*: cf. I. 31. 16 *cichorea levesque malvae.*

2. **pater**, Juppiter, as in III. 29. 44.

3. **arces**, the two summits of the Capitoline, called Capitolium and Arx.

5. **gentis**, 'mankind,' as in I. 3. 28.

6. **Pyrrhae**, who, with her husband Deucalion, alone survived the great mythical flood (described in Ovid, *Metam.* I. 260–450).

nova monstra, 'horrors unknown before.'

7. Proteus, a sea-god who kept the herd of seals belonging to Poseidon. He is described in Verg. *Georg.* IV. 429–435 and in Homer, *Od.* IV. 446 sqq.

8. visere, see *Introd.* p. xxiii.

9. haesit, 'was entangled.'

14. litore Etrusco, 'from the shore of the Etruscan sea,' as in *C.S.* 38 and *Epod.* 16. 40. It is sometimes interpreted 'from the Etruscan (i.e. the right) bank of the river.'

15. regis, sc. Numae.

monumenta...Vestae. The temple of Vesta, the house of the Vestal virgins and the *regia*, or house of the Pontifex Maximus, stood, adjoining one another, on the west side of the Via Sacra just at the point where floods would break in. All these buildings were ascribed to Numa Pompilius.

Julius Caesar lived in the *regia*, and there was undoubtedly a great flood in the spring or winter of B.C. 44, the year when he was murdered. It is not likely, however, that Hor. is alluding to this flood, which happened when he was a student in Athens and long before he could have written this ode.

17. Iliae, the supposed ancestress of the *Iulia gens.* She was the daughter of Aeneas and sister of Iulus. According to one legend, she (and not Rea Silvia) was the mother of Romulus. After his birth, she was flung into the Tiber (or the Anio, according to Ovid), but the river-god rescued her and made her his wife.

nimium, probably with *se iactat* (so Kiessling), though most edd. take it with *querenti.* But Ilia has a right to complain loudly. It is Tiber who shows unnecessary violence.

querenti, complaining of the murder of Julius Caesar.

18. iactat se Iliae, 'vaunts himself in the eyes of Ilia as her avenger.' For the construction, cf. Ovid *Her.* XII. 175 *stultae dum te iactare maritae quaeris.*

19. Iove non probante. Porphyrion explains: *quod terreri Iuppiter populum iusserit, non perire.*

19, 20. uxorius amnis. Division of a word between the third and fourth lines of a Sapphic stanza occurs also in I. 25. 11 and in II. 16. 7. Sappho has it several times in the few extant specimens of her poetry, and it seems clear that, in the original rhythm, the fourth line was continuous with the third, so that the stanza consisted of three lines only.

21. audiet...ferrum. The subject is *iuventus* in v. 24. The line is commonly interpreted 'will hear how citizens sharpened the sword *against each other*,' the sense being brought out partly by the emphasis on *cives* and partly by the mention of a better purpose in the next line. But a passage in Ovid (*Metam.* XV. 775) where Venus, pleading for the life of Julius Caesar, says '*en acui sceleratos cernitis enses?*' suggests that the allusion here is to the murder of Julius.

NOTES. 43

civis, cf. Tac. *Hist.* II. 38 *non discessere ab armis in Pharsalia ac Philippis civium legiones.*

22. **graves Persae.** 'The Parthian pest.' The Parthians (called also *Medi* in v. 51), a semi-barbarous people living in the region south of the Caspian sea, had defeated Crassus and captured his standards at Carrhae, B.C. 53. The Romans had not yet succeeded in retrieving this disaster, which rankled in their memory.

perirent. The opinion expressed is Horace's, therefore the tense is imperf. not pluperf.

24. **rara,** 'thinned by their fathers' fault.'

25. **vocet,** 'what god shall the people invoke?': the jussive subj. converted into a question. (Roby, *L. G.* § 1610: Goodwin, *G. M. & T.* § 288.)

26. **rebus,** dat. 'to help the fortunes.'

27. **minus audientem carmina,** 'deaf to their hymns.' *minus* is really negative as in *quo minus,* cf. *parum* in I. 12. 59.

29. **partis,** properly an actor's 'part.'

scelus, guilt that involves pollution: such as parricide and fratricide.

31. **nube...amictus,** copied from Homer (*Il.* V. 186) νεφέλῃ εἰλυμένος ὤμους.

32. **augur Apollo.** The gods invoked are all specially connected with Julius Caesar. He was the priest of Vesta: his ancestor Cn. Julius dedicated the only temple to Apollo then existing in Rome (Livy, IV. 29): Venus was his mythical ancestress: Mars his mythical ancestor.

Apollo is described as *augur* in *Carm. Saec.* 61 and in Verg., *Aen.* IV. 376. The title was not known to the Greeks.

33-35. **sive...sive.** The apodosis is *venias,* repeated from v. 30. 'Come, if thou wilt, smiling Venus.'

Erycina, Venus, who had a famous temple on Mt Eryx in Sicily.

36. **auctor,** Mars, 'founder' of the Julian line and Roman nation, cf. Verg. *Aen.* IV. 365 *generis nec Dardanus auctor.*

39. **Mauri peditis.** See Critical Note.

41. **sive.** The apodosis is *serus...redeas* in v. 45.

iuvenem. Octavianus was born B.C. 63, and was a young man at any date which can reasonably be assigned to the ode.

43. **filius Maiae,** i.e. Mercurius. (Nom. for Voc.)

patiens...ultor. Octavian frequently declared that his sole purpose in entering on civil war was to avenge his (adoptive) father's murder. On the field of Philippi (B.C. 42) he vowed a temple to Mars Ultor, and in his address to the senate on Jan. 1st, B.C. 27, he declared that he resigned his powers to show that he had never desired empire for himself, but only 'to avenge his father cruelly slain and to rescue the state from great mischiefs' (Dion Cass. LIII. 4). It is the first of his exploits commemorated on the Monumentum Ancyranum: 'Qui parentem meum interfecerant, eos in exilium expuli iudiciis legitimis ultus eorum facinus, et postea bellum inferentis rei publicae **vici** bis acie.'

47. **n. v. iniquum**, 'intolerant of' (Wickham).

49. **triumphos**. He celebrated a triple triumph on the 6th, 7th and 8th of Aug. B.C. 29, for victories in Pannonia, at Actium and in Egypt.

50. **pater**, as a god, cf. *Bacche pater* in I. 18. 6. The formal title *pater patriae* was not given to Augustus till B.C. 2.

princeps. He became *princeps senatus* in B.C. 29, but it is now a generally accepted doctrine that *princeps* does not mean *princeps senatus*, but was a mere title of respect addressed to the 'foremost citizen' of Rome. (Cf. Tac. *Ann.* I. 1 *cuncta discordiis civilibus fessa nomine principis sub imperium accepit.*) The title had been previously used of Pompey and of Julius Caesar, and Cicero had suggested the appointment of a *princeps civitatis* to heal existing dissensions. Cf. II. 1. 4 and see article *Princeps* in Smith's *Dic. of Antiq.* 3rd ed., and Pelham's *Hist. of Rome*, p. 370.

51. **Medos**. The Parthians, whom Hor. identified with the Persians (v. 22), and therefore (in the Greek manner) with the Medes.

52. **te duce**, 'while thou art *our* leader.' The words would naturally imply that Caesar was leader of the Medes.

Ode III.

The Ode is a *propempticon* or 'god-speed' to the ship which was conveying Vergil the poet to Athens. The only known voyage of Vergil to Athens was in B.C. 19, just before his death; but the ode must have been written earlier than that (*Introd.* p. xvii). See Nettleship in Conington's Vergil, I. p. xxiv.

The *propempticon* seems to have been a favourite form of composition with Alexandrian poets. There is one in Theocritus (VII. 52, sqq.), and the beginning of one by Callimachus is preserved. Statius (*Silvae* III. 2) wrote one in imitation of this ode.

Scheme. Ship, if thou carriest my Vergil safe, then may all the gods preserve thee. What a courage that man had who first ventured to brave the dangers of the deep! But there are no limits to the impious audacity of mortals. We scale heaven itself and provoke the just wrath of Juppiter.

Metre. The third Asclepiad (*Introd.* p. xxx).

1. **sic**. Editors cite many passages apparently parallel (see Lewis and Short s. v. v. 1) to show that *sic* here must mean 'on this condition.' (Cf. I. 28. 25.) The condition is stated later, vv. 7, 8 *reddas...et serves.* For the order, cf. Vergil *Ecl.* 9. 30 *Sic tua Cyrneas fugiant examina taxos...Incipe.* In effect, vv. 1-8 would thus mean 'O ship, preserve my Vergil: so may the gods preserve thee.'

The construction appears at first sight to be illogical, because the ship could not preserve Vergil unless she were herself preserved. But it

NOTES. 45

becomes logical enough, if we suppose Vergil was already ill when he went on shipboard, and Horace was afraid that he might not survive the voyage. If Vergil died at sea, Horace did not care what became of the ship.

diva. Venus, whose most famous shrine was at Paphos in Cyprus (cf. I. 30. 1, 2): she was invoked by Phoenician sailors and is thus called *marina* in III. 26. 5, IV. 11. 15.

potens Cypri: cf. *potenti maris deo* in I. 5. 15 and I. 6. 10.

2. **fratres Helenae.** Castor and Pollux, to whom were attributed the lights (called 'St Elmo's fires') which sometimes appear on the masts of a vessel in times of electrical disturbance. These lights (and not the constellation Gemini) are the *lucida sidera*. This is clear from Pliny, *N. H.* II. 101, and from the imitation of this ode by Statius (*Silvae* III. 7. 8) *proferte benigna Sidera et antennae gemino considite cornu.*

3. **ventorum pater.** Aeolus. See Homer, *Od.* X. 19 sqq.

regat, sing. though there are three nominatives, cf. *erat* in v. 10.

4. **aliis,** 'all the rest.'

Iapyga, a north-west wind blowing from the Iapygian Promontorium in Apulia towards Greece. It is called *albus* 'clearing' in III. 27. 20.

6. **debes.** Kiessling, following the suggestion of Porphyrion, construes *debes finibus Att.* together.

7. **reddas.** Jussive, as *remittas* and *trepides* in II. 11. 3, 4.

8. **animae dim.,** cf. *te meae partem animae* in II. 17. 5. Hor. had a strong affection for Vergil and Varius, who introduced him to Maecenas. In *Sat.* I. 5. 40, 41 he speaks of them as *animae quales neque candidiores Terra tulit neque queis me sit devinctior alter.*

9. **robur et aes triplex.** The 'oak and triple brass' are not to be conceived as armour, but as the material of which the man's ribs are made.

10, 11. **fragilem truci...pelago ratem.** The placing of the words is peculiarly Horatian: cf. vv. 14, 22, 28, of the first ode.

12. **Africum,** S.W. wind.

13. **decertantem,** 'fighting to the death': cf. *deproeliantes* in I. 9. 11: *debellata* III. 3. 55.

Aquilonibus, N.E. wind. (For the dat. cf. I. 1. 15.)

14. **tristis,** 'gloomy': *pluvias Hyadas* Verg. *Aen.* III. 516. The Hyades are a cluster in the constellation Taurus. The ancients derived the name from ὕειν 'to rain,' but it seems likely to mean 'piglings' (just as *Pleiades*, commonly derived from πλεῖν 'to sail,' seems likely to mean 'flock of pigeons'). The time (end of November) when the Hyades set at sunrise ushered in the stormiest period of the year. See art. *Astronomia* in Smith's *Dict. of Ant.*

Noti, the Greek name for the S. wind, called in Latin *auster* (*dux inquieti turbidus Hadriae* III. 3. 5).

15. **arbiter,** 'than whom there is no mightier ruler of the Adriatic.'

16. tollere. The first *seu* is omitted, as in Sat. II. 8. 16 *Albanum, Maecenas, sive Falernum Te magis appositis delectat, habemus utrumque.*
ponere, 'to lull.'

17. gradum, 'stride.' The word is often used of a fighting attitude, e.g. *inque gradu stetimus, certi non cedere,* Ov. *Metam.* IX. 43.

18. siccis, 'tearless.' The ancient Greeks, as every reader of Homer knows, wept freely from fear or other emotions. The impassive behaviour of the modern Englishman seems to have been only gradually acquired. See the description of the scene which preceded the murder of Becket in Stanley's *Memorials of Canterbury,* p. 56.

20. Acroceraunia (now Cape Glossa), a cliff on the coast of Epirus, *infamis* for shipwrecks.

22. prudens emphatic, as in III. 29. 29.

dissociabili with active sense, 'estranging' (as Matt. Arnold 'the unplumb'd salt estranging sea'): but Statius in his imitation (*Silvae* III. 2. 61) speaks of the sea as *rude et abscissum miseris animantibus,* from which it may be inferred that he took *dissoc.* here in the passive sense as 'estranged.' Adjs. in *-bilis* are not often active in Hor., but he has *illacrymabilis* 'unable to weep' in II. 14. 6 and *flebilis* 'weeping' in IV. 2. 21. *Penetrabile frigus* in Verg. *Georg.* I. 93 and *genitabilis aura Favoni* in Lucretius I. 11 are good specimens.

25. audax...perpeti, cf. *Introd.* p. xxiii.

26. gens humana. The audacious ingenuity of man is the theme of one of the most famous passages of Sophocles (*Antig.* 333 sqq.).

27. audax. For the repetition cf. I. 2. 4, 5 and 21, 23.
Iapeti genus. Prometheus son of Iapetus.

28. fraude mala, 'an unhappy theft' (Wickham).

30. macies, 'wasting sickness.'

31. incubuit, 'attacked,' cf. Lucr. VI. 1141 *morbifer aestus Incubuit populo Pandionis.*

32. prius with *semoti.*

necessitas with *leti* 'doom of death.' In the golden age (as described by Hesiod *Works and Days* 90 sqq.) men lived untroubled by disease and died as if falling asleep. Conington translates 'and slow fate quicken'd Death's once halting pace,' separating *necessitas* from *leti.*

34. expertus for *expertus est.*

36. perrupit Acheronta. The final *-it* is lengthened by the rhythmical accent or stress, commonly (but erroneously) called *arsis.* (The word *arsis* 'raising' originally meant 'lifting the foot' and so 'removing the stress,' not 'raising the voice.') Other examples are II. 6. 14 *angulus ridet ubi:* II. 13. 16 *timet aliunde* and III. 16. 26 *quicquid arat impiger.*

Herculeus labor, 'the labour of Hercules,' cf. *Herculea manu* in II. 12. 6 and *Giganteo triumpho* in III. 1. 7 (where *Giganteo* represents an objective genitive). See Roby *L. G.* § 1277.

37. **ardui.** For the gen. cf. *Epp.* II. I. 31 *nil intra est oleam, nil extra est in nuce duri.*

40. **iracunda.** The epithet belongs really to Juppiter, cf. *incontinentes manus* in I. 17. 26: *dementes ruinas* in I. 37. 7.

Ode IV.

To Sestius, who is probably L. Sestius, a member of the conservative (or republican) party, who had served with Horace under Brutus. He was consul for the latter half of B.C. 23.

Scheme. Spring is come again, with all its delights. But do not hope that it will last for ever. Death comes to all of us and after death there are no more pleasures.

Metre. The Fourth or Greater Archilochian, used by Hor. in this ode only. (Cf. *Introd.* p. xxxi.) The metre is used in some extant fragments of Archilochus and seems to have been frequently imitated by Alexandrian poets.

1. **solvitur,** cf. *dissolve frigus* in I. 9. 5. Frost is regarded as a fetter. We have the same metaphor in the expression 'frost-bound.'

grata vice, abl. of the instr. 'with welcome change,' cf. the construction of *mutare* in I. 17. 2, and *mutat terra vices* in IV. 7. 3.

vice veris et Favoni. The repetition of *v* (pronounced as a labial *w*) seems to suggest the whisper of the breeze. But it often suggests the *whistling* of a stormy wind, as in *ventorum validis viribus.* See Munro's introductory notes to *Lucr.* p. 15.

siccas. The ships have been hauled up 'high and dry' for the winter.

2. **machinae,** 'windlasses' employed with rollers, *phalangae.*

5. **Cytherea Venus.** The adj., so emphatically placed, is perhaps equivalent to 'in Cythera.' It is unusual to find the name of a deity coupled with a geographical limitation: cf. III. 4. 64 *Delius et Patareus Apollo.*

6. **iunctaeque N. G.,** cf. IV. 7. 5 *Gratia cum Nymphis geminisque sororibus.*

7, 8. **gravis officinas,** under Aetna and the Lipari isles, where the Cyclopes were busy forging the thunderbolts of Zeus. *graves* means 'deafening' or 'scorching' or in some other way 'unbearable.'

ardens, 'glowing' either with the heat or with the reflection of the fire.

9. **nitidum,** 'shining' with ointment. Cf. II. 7. 7 *nitentes malobathro Syrio capillos.*

10. **solutae,** cf. *v.* 1 and Verg. *Georg.* I. 44 *Zephyro putris se glaeba resolvit.*

11. **Faunus,** an Italian god, identified by Roman poets with the Greek Pan. He was worshipped in Rome especially on the 13th and

15th of February and was supposed to govern the fertility both of crops and of herds.

12. **agna...haedo.** Supply *sibi immolari*. Verbs of sacrificing may take an instr. abl. of the thing sacrificed: cf. Verg. *Ecl.* 3. 77 *cum faciam vitula pro frugibus, ipse venito.* Livy XLI. 14 *immolare Iovi singulis bubus.* For the ellipse of *sibi immolari* cf. the ellipse of *ludere* in III. 24. 57.

13. **aequo,** 'impartial.'

pulsat, sc. pede. Cf. Plaut. *Most.* 453 *pulsando pedibus paene confregi hasce ambas (fores).* The alliteration is imitative of the noise.

14. **regum,** 'the great' as in II. 14. 11 *sive reges sive inopes erimus coloni.*

15. **summa,** 'span' (i.e. total extent). Some scholars insist that *brevis* is gen. agreeing with *vitae.*

longam, 'far-reaching.' Cf. I. 11. 6 *spatio brevi spem longam reseces.*

16. **iam,** 'in due time.' Cf. II. 5. 10 and 20. 13.

premet, 'will hem thee round.'

fabulaeque manes. It seems plain from Persius (5. 151 *cinis et manes et fabula fies*) that *fabulae* is in apposition with *manes. Fabulae* seems to mean 'things that are merely talked of,' hence 'unsubstantial.' Schütz thinks *fabulae* is gen.=*fabulosi,* as we might say 'the ghosts of story' or 'storied ghosts.'

17. **exilis,** 'bare.' Cf. *Epp.* I. 6. 45 *exilis domus est ubi non et multa supersunt.* Some critics interpret 'narrow,' as if the *domus Plut.* were the grave: or 'thin,' i.e. shadowy, unsubstantial.

Plutonia, cf. *Herculeus labor* in 3.

simul mearis=*simul ac meaveris.*

18. **regna vini sortiere talis,** 'you will not choose with dice the ruler of the revel.' Cf. II. 7. 25 *quem Venus arbitrum dicet bibendi?* where he who makes the throw called 'Venus' is chosen. The duty of the *rex* or symposiarch was to determine the amount and the strength of the wine and impose forfeits on those who disobeyed his commands. See *Symposium* in Smith's *Dict. of Antiq.*

talis, 'knuckle-bones,' ἀστράγαλοι.

19. **mirabere,** 'admire.'

quo, instr. abl.

calet, 'is hotly in love': *tepebunt* in 20 implies a more modest passion.

Ode V.

To Pyrrha, a 'light o' love' lady. She is not elsewhere addressed and very likely was not a real person.

Scheme. Who is now your lover, Pyrrha? Poor boy, he trusts you entirely, not knowing that your love is fickle and treacherous, like the summer sea. Once you made shipwreck of me, but I escaped with my life.

Metre. Fifth Asclepiad (*Introd.* p. xxx).

1. **multa in rosa,** 'on heaped-up rose-leaves.'

gracilis, 'slim.'

2. **urget,** 'woos.'

3. **Pyrrha,** the Greek πυρρά, means 'yellow-haired.' Hence *flavam* in 4.

antro, 'grotto,' an artificial cave.

4. **religas,** 'tie back.' Cf. *incomptum Lacaenae more comae religata nodum* in II. 11. 23.

5. **simplex munditiis,** 'plain in thy neatness' (Milton), but *munditiae* is rather 'elegance' than 'neatness.'

6. **mutatos** belongs in sense to both *fidem* and *deos* (cf. *dirae* I. 2. 1): 'thy perfidy and his own adverse fates.'

7. **nigris,** 'darkening' as *niger Eurus* in *Epod.* 10. 5. On the other hand *candidus* or *albus* applied to a wind means 'clearing': as in I. 7. 15 and III. 7. 1.

8. **emirabitur,** 'will be astounded at.' The verb is only found here and is obviously intended to express intense wonder. Cf. *evitata* in I. 1. 5 n.

insolens, 'unused to them.' Cf. Sallust *Cat.* 3 *insolens malarum artium.*

9. **credulus aurea.** The juxtaposition of the adjectives throws emphasis on each. Cf. *tenues grandia* in I. 6. 10.

10. **vacuam.** In I. 6. 19 *vacui* means 'fancy-free.' Here *vacuam* must mean 'free from new fancies' and so devoted to her lover.

11. **aurae,** the breeze of caprice: as in *arbitrio popularis aurae* III. 2. 20. But the word suggests the following metaphor.

13. **nites.** The metaphor (as in *aurea* l. 9) seems to be from a smooth sea shining and sparkling in the sunlight.

14. **tabula votiva.** Sailors, in danger of shipwreck, used to invoke the aid of some deity, usually one whose temple was near. In this temple, if they escaped, they would dedicate the clothes they had worn, together with a tablet recording their thanks to the deity. In *Aen.* XII. 766 Vergil mentions a wild olive at Laurentum, sacred to Faunus, on which shipwrecked sailors *figere dona solebant Laurenti divo et votas suspendere vestes.* Neptune, no doubt, received most of such offerings. The tablet often bore a picture of the shipwreck. See Mayor on Juvenal XII. 27.

15. **potenti** with *maris,* as *potens Cypri* in 3. 1.

16. **deo,** sc. *Neptuno.*

The following translation is an early work, perhaps a college exercise (about 1625), of John Milton:

What slender youth, bedew'd with liquid odours,
Courts thee on roses in some pleasant cave,
  Pyrrha? For whom bind'st thou
  In wreaths thy golden hair,
Plain in thy neatness? O, how oft shall he
On faith and changed gods complain, and seas
  Rough with black winds, and storms
  Unwonted shall admire!
Who now enjoys thee credulous, all gold,
Who always vacant, always amiable,
  Hopes thee, of flattering gales
  Unmindful. Hapless they,
To whom thou untried seem'st fair! Me, in my vow'd
Picture, the sacred wall declares to have hung
  My dank and dropping weeds
  To the stern god of sea.

Ode VI.

To M. Vipsanius Agrippa, the celebrated general and friend of Augustus. (See note on l. 3.) He was consul three times (B.C. 37, 28, 27): married Aug.'s daughter Julia in B.C. 21 and died in 13 B.C. He seems to have asked Horace to celebrate his exploits in an epic poem.

Scheme. Varius shall sing your feats of arms, Agrippa. I cannot and dare not try to celebrate such glorious deeds. What lyrist is fit to sing of the heroic figures of epic poetry? Wine and love are the themes of my muse. (For a similar treatment of a similar subject cf. II. 12 and IV. 2.)

Metre. The Fourth Asclepiad.

1. **scriberis.** A permissive future, like *laudabunt alii* in I. 7. 1. 'You can get Varius to write about you.' As a matter of fact, Varius did write a *Panegyricus Augusti*, which must have contained much about Agrippa.

Vario...aliti. The MS. reading *alite* is defended by Orelli as abl. abs. ('Varius being the bird of Maeonian song'), but *alite* is too far removed from *Vario* and the abl. abs. is not emphatic enough to contrast with *nos* of l. 5.

The alteration *scribere ab Vario* is not permissible, for Hor. does not use *ab* with the agent anywhere in the lyrics and very rarely elsewhere (*Sat.* I. 2. 11: 5. 92: 6. 88: 7. 22: *Epist.* I. 1. 103: 12. 3: are the only instances and some of these are doubtful).

Some editors regard *alite* as instrum. abl. used for abl. of the agent, but no clear parallel can be cited. Vergil's *uno graditur comitatus Achate* (*Aen.* I. 312) is not similar, for the abl. is usual with *comitatus*, even in prose. Other instances of abl. without *ab* (e.g. *Epist.* I. 1. 94 *curatus inaequali tonsore* or *Sat.* II. 1. 84 *iudice laudatus Caesare*) are complicated by the presence of an adj. or noun in apposition, and are usually regarded as abl. abs. (See Munro's note in Mayor's *Juvenal* at I. 13 *assiduo ruptae lectore columnae.*)

The dative *aliti*, which is the only alternative, is confirmed by *Epist*. I. 19. 3 *carmina quae scribuntur aquae potoribus* and *Sat*. I. 10. 15 *illi scripta quibus comoedia prisca viris est*, where *potoribus* and *viris* are, almost beyond question, dative. But the dative of the agent with *simple* tenses passive is uncommon even in poetry. Vergil's *neque cernitur ulli* (*Aen*. I. 440) and Ovid's *non intelligor ulli* (*Trist*. V. 10. 35) are not good instances, the dat. here being partly that of 'the person interested.'

Varlo. L. Varius Rufus (about B.C. 74-14) was an intimate friend of Vergil and afterwards of Horace whom he introduced to Maecenas. He was regarded at this time as the chief epic poet of Rome, Vergil being known only as the author of the Eclogues and the Georgics. In *Sat*. I. 10. 51 Horace says *forte epos acer ut nemo Varius ducit*. He wrote epics on Julius Caesar and Augustus (two lines of his are quoted in *Epist*. I. 16. 27, 28) and a very popular tragedy entitled *Thyestes*. He and Tucca were Vergil's literary executors, who saved the *Aeneid* from destruction.

2. **Maeonii**, i.e. Homeric, for Homer was said to have been born in Maeonia (Lydia). For the gen. cf. III. 7. 4 *constantis iuvenem fidei*.

aliti. Cf. *Dircaeum cycnum* applied to Pindar in IV. 2.

3. **quam rem cumque.** For the separation (*tmesis*) of *quam* from *cumque* cf. I. 7. 25 and 9. 14.

navibus aut equis. Of Agrippa's military feats the most famous were the capture of Perusia B.C. 40 and the conquest of Aquitania B.C. 38. Of his naval battles the chief were those of Mylae and Naulochus in B.C. 36 and Actium in B.C. 31.

6. **Pelidae stomachum.** the wrath of Achilles: μῆνιν Πηληιάδεω Ἀχιλῆος, *Iliad* I. I. For *stomachum* cf. I. 16. 16.

7. **duplicis**, 'wily.' πολύτροπος or πολύμητις are the stock epithets of Odysseus in Homer.

Ulixei. This gen. (cf. *Achillei* in I. 15. 34) is formed as if the nom. were *Ulixeus*, though that nom. is not found in Latin. (See Roby *Lat. Gr.* § 482.) The Lat. *Ulixes* (for Gk. 'Οδυσσεύς) is said to be borrowed from a Doric dialect of Magna Graecia. For the *x*, cf. Latin *Ajax*, *Ajacis* with Greek Αἴας, Αἴαντος, *malaxo* with μαλάσσω, etc.

8. **saevam Pelopis domum.** Apparently an allusion to Varius' tragedy of 'Thyestes,' published in B.C. 30.

9. **tenues grandia.** For the emphasis given by juxtaposition cf. *perfidus hospitam* in I. 15. 2.

10. **lyrae potens**, cf. I. 3. 1.

vetat. For the number cf. I. 3. 10.

13. **quis**, i.e. what *lyric* poet, for it would be absurd to deny that Homer or even Varius had written worthily on such themes.

tunica...adamantina. χαλκοχίτων, *Iliad* I. 371. *adamas* is the hardest steel. Cf. III. 24. 5.

14. **pulvere—nigrum.** Cf. *pulvere sordidos* in II. 1. 21.

4—2

52   HORACE, ODES I. vi, vii.

16. Tydiden. Diomedes, who, at the instigation of Pallas Athene, wounded Ares and Aphrodite in battle. *Iliad* v. 881–884.

18. sectis, 'pared' so that they do not hurt. Bentley proposed *strictis*, as if *unguibus* were substituted in joke for *ensibus*. He compares Ovid *Am.* I. 6. 14 *non timeo strictas in mea fata manus* and Statius *Theb.* III. 537 (of eagles) *strictis unguibus instant.*

19. vacui, 'fancy-free.'

20. non praeter=*secundum,* 'according to my wont.'

leves, 'light-hearted.'

Ode VII.

To L. Munatius Plancus (born about B.C. 85), who served as legatus of Julius Caesar in Gaul, was consul B.C. 42, and governed Asia and Syria for Antony but ultimately joined Octavian. It was he who proposed in the senate that Octavian should receive the *cognomen* ot *Augustus* (B.C. 27).

Scheme. Other poets may celebrate other places, but I love Tibur best of all. Plancus, when you are at Tibur, do not forget the soothing influence of wine. Teucer, when he fared forth into exile, drowned his sorrows in wine.

[The transitions in this Ode are so abrupt that many readers in ancient times divided it into two poems, consisting of ll. 1–14 and 15–32. It would seem that Plancus was going to Tibur for a holiday and that he was suffering from some illness or anxiety for which wine was, in Horace's judgment, a good remedy.]

Metre. The Alcmanian strophe, consisting of dactylic hexameters and tetrameters. (The metre is used again only in I. 28 and *Epod.* 12.)

1. laudabunt. The permissive future (cf. I. 6. 1)=*laudent licet,* cf. *linquet* in III. 23. 12 and Vergil *Aen.* VI. 848 *excudent alii spirantia mollius aera,...tu regere imperio populos, Romane, memento.*

claram, 'sunny.' Cf. Pliny *N. H.* II. 62 *Rhodi et Syracusis nunquam tanta nubila obduci ut non aliqua hora sol cernatur.*

aut...aut. Three eastern places are distinguished with *aut,* then three western places are distinguished with *ve* or *vel,* but *vel* is not used with Tempe apparently because Tempe is also *locus insignis Apolline.*

3. Baccho...Apolline, abl. of the means with *insignis,* like *clari giganteo triumpho* in III. 1. 7.

4. Tempe. A Greek neut. plur. indeclinable. For the connexion of Tempe with Apollo cf. I. 21. 9.

5. sunt quibus...est, cf. I. 1. 3.

intactae, 'virgin.' Cf. *integra Diana* in III. 4. 70.

Palladis urbem. Athens.

6. carmine perpetuo, 'an unbroken strain,' i.e. a long continuous composition. Thus Ovid (*Metam.* I. 4) speaks of his *Metamorphoses* (about 12000 lines) as *perpetuum carmen.*

7. undique...olivam. The poet assumes the garland of the god whom he celebrates. Thus the poet of wine wears the ivy of Bacchus (III. 25. 20) and the poet of love wears the myrtle of Venus (cf. I. 38. 5 and Ovid *Am.* I. 1. 29). So he who sings of Pallas, will wear the olive which was sacred to Pallas Athena, who created it.

undique decerptam probably means 'plucked from every spot,' as if the poet celebrated every nook and corner of Athenian soil. The version 'plucked by everybody' is not suitable, for the point of the lines is that only *some* poets celebrate Athens.

8. plurimus, in the sense of *plurimi,* is not found elsewhere without a subst. (e.g. *plurimus oleaster* Vergil *Georg.* II. 182): but there is one clear instance of *multus = multi* in Lucan (*Phars.* III. 707 *multus sua vulnera puppi affixit moriens*). Many scholars, however, reading *plurimus in I. honore* translate 'he who is devoted to the honour of Juno,' comparing such expressions as *totus in illis* (*nugis*) *Sat.* I. 9. 2, *omnis in hoc sum Ep.* I. 1. 11, *multus esse in re nota* Cic. *de Or.* II. 87.

in honorem. Cf. Livy II. 27. 6 *quod facile apparebat non tam ad honorem eius factum.* Quintilian XI. 2. 12 *in honorem victoriae.*

9. aptum equis, ἱππόβοτον Ἄργος in *Iliad* II. 287.

ditis, πολύχρυσος Μυκήνη in *Iliad* VII. 180. In *Iliad* IV. 51 Hera declares that the cities dearest to her are Argos, Sparta and Mycenae.

10. patiens Lacedaemon, 'hardy Sparta' is contrasted with wealthy Larissa (called ἐριβῶλαξ 'loamy' in *Iliad* II. 841).

12—14. domus...rivis. These lines name four chief attractions of Tibur, viz. the grotto or temple of Albunea the Sibyl, the falls of the Anio, the grove of Tiburnus the founder of Tibur, and the orchards watered by canals or by the rapids below the falls (*pomosis Anio qua spumifer incubat arvis,* Prop. **v.** 7. 81)

12. Albuneae resonantis. Albunea, properly the name of the Sibyl, is here applied to her temple or grotto, which 'echoes' with the roar of the falls. So Verg. *Aen.* VII. 82 speaks of another Albunea, *nemorum quae maxima sacro fonte sonat.*

15. albus, 'clearing': so *albus Iapyx* in III. 27. 19: *candidi Favonii* in III. 7. 1: *alba stella* in I. 12. 27.

17. sapiens finire memento. For the advice cf. I. 11. 6 *sapias, vina liques.* Also II. 11. 7, III. 21. 17, *Epod.* 9. 37.

19. molli mero, 'mellow wine.'

20. tenebit, 'holds you, as it soon will.' The scholiast Porphyrion says that Plancus was born in Tibur.

21. Teucer was a son of Telamon, king of Salamis, and a half-brother of Ajax, whom he accompanied to the Trojan war. When Ajax was disgraced and committed suicide, Teucer returned home but was disowned by his father because he had not avenged his brother's wrongs. Cf. Euripides *Helena* 87-97, Soph. *Ajax* 1008 sq., Cic. *de Or.* II. 46. 93 (quoting the *Teucer* of Pacuvius).

22. cum fugeret, 'when he was leaving Salamis for ever.'

uda Lyaeo tempora, 'temples moist with wine.' Similar expressions are not uncommon: e.g. *multo perfusum tempora Baccho* in Tibullus (I. 2. 3): and it would seem that they may be taken literally, though *udus* and *uvidus* sometimes mean 'tipsy' (as in II. 19. 18, IV. 5. 39). Perhaps the garlands of drinkers were dipped in wine.

23. populea. The poplar was sacred to Hercules, the wanderer (*vagus* III. 3. 9) and the guide of wanderers (ἡγεμών, Xen. *Anab.* IV. 8. 25).

25. quo...cumque. Cf. I. 6. 3. A proverbial saying *patria est ubicumque est bene* was ascribed to Teucer (Cic. *Tusc.* v. 37. 108).

27. T. duce et auspice T., abl. abs. A Roman commander was usually *dux* and *auspex* to his troops (cf. *qui ductu auspicioque eius rem prospere gesserant,* Livy v. 46. 6): though sometimes a superior magistrate took the auspices on opening a campaign, leaving the command of it to a subordinate.

The word *auspex* properly means 'one who watches the birds' and takes auspices, but it often means the god who *gives* auspices, the 'patron' of the undertaking (e.g. *auspice Musa* in *Epist.* I. 3. 13). Hence some editors read here *auspice Teucri,* rendering the words 'under the guidance of Teucer and Teucer's patron (Apollo).'

28. certus, 'unerring,' νημερτής.

29. ambiguam...Salamina, 'a Salamis to dispute the name' (Wickham). The Salamis founded by Teucer was in Cyprus.

30. peioraque passi, cf. Verg. *Aen.* I. 199 *o passi graviora, dabit deus his quoque finem.*

32. iterabimus, 'we will plough again' (cf. I. 34. 4). Teucer had just returned from Troy.

Ode VIII.

To Lydia, another 'light o' love,' who is addressed also in I. 18 and III. 9.

Scheme. Lydia, you are ruining the life of Sybaris. He, who was so famous an athlete, is seen no more in the field. You keep him in hiding as Thetis kept Achilles.

Metre. Greater Sapphic (*Introd.* p. xxx), not used again by Horace.

4. campum, the Campus Martius, where Roman youths practised military sports.

patiens, 'though fit to endure.' Cf. Juv. VII. 33 *aetas et pelagi patiens et cassidis atque ligonis.* For the omission of *quamvis* cf. I. 32. 6 (*ferox bello*).

5. militaris, nom. sing. 'as a soldier': not acc. plur.

6. Gallica ora. The Romans preferred the horses of Gaul, and many of the Roman 'horsey' terms are Gallic: e.g. *mannus, caballus, petorritum, essedum, Epona.*

lupatis, 'jagged' like wolves' teeth. Cf. Ovid *Am.* I. 3. 15 *asper equus duris contunditur ora lupatis.*

8. **olivum,** the oil with which athletes anointed themselves.

9. **sanguine viperino,** considered a deadly poison. Cf. *Epod.* 3. 6.

10. **livida armis,** 'black and blue with the weapons,' probably the boxing-gloves, though they are not mentioned. Possibly, however, *livida* refers to the swollen veins of the arm.

11. **saepe...expedito,** 'famed as he was for hurling the quoit often and the javelin too beyond the mark.'

14. **filium Thetidis.** Achilles, whose mother disguised him as a girl and sent him to Scyros, in order that he might escape service in the Trojan war. Ulysses, however, discovered him. (Ovid, *Metam.* XIII. 162 sqq.)

sub, 'just before,' as in *sub noctem.*

16. **cultus,** 'a man's dress.' Cf. Livy XXIX. 19. 11 *militaris cultus.*

Lycias. The Lycians under Glaucus and Sarpedon were allies of the Trojans.

Ode IX.

To Thaliarchus, an imaginary youth.

Scheme. It is cold, Thaliarchus. Heap up the logs and bring out the wine. Make yourself comfortable in the present and take no thought for the future. Youth is the time for dancing and wooing and sporting with the lasses.

Parts of this ode are imitated from an ode of Alcaeus of which we have fragments (*Introd.* p. xxxviii).

Metre. Alcaic stanza (*Introd.* p. xxvii).

2. **Soracte,** a conspicuous mountain about 25 miles north of Rome. It is now called S. Oreste.

3. **laborantes,** 'groaning.'

4. **constiterint,** cf. Ovid *Trist.* V. 10. 1 *frigore constitit Ister.* The Tiber is very rarely frozen over. The image of frozen streams is borrowed from Alcaeus, who must often have seen them in Thrace.

acuto, 'piercing.'

5. **dissolve,** cf. I. 4. 1.

6. **benignius,** more liberally than usual.

7, 8. **deprome...diota,** 'draw the four-year-old wine from the Sabine jar.' Cf. *Epod.* 2. 47 *promens dolio. Depromere* is also used in the sense of bringing out a jar from the cellar (cf. I. 37. 5).

quadrimum merum. The age of wine is indicated by these adjectives: *hornum* (this year's), *bimum* (last year's), *trimum, quadrimum, quinquenne,* etc.

Sabina diota. A *diota,* or 'two-eared' jar, is doubtless the same thing as an amphora (ἀμφορεύς = ἀμφι-φορεύς 'two-handled'). A Sabine jar would contain Sabine wine, just as a Laestrygonian jar (III. 16. 34) contains Formian. Sabine wine was cheap (I. 20. 1).

9. **qui simul**=*nam simul atque illi.*

11. **deproeliantis**, 'fighting it out on the boiling sea.' Cf. *decertantem* in I. 3. 13.

cupressi, tall trees growing on the plain.

12. **veteres orni**, gnarled old rowan trees on the hillside.

13. **quid sit futurum.** This is the advice of an Epicurean (*Epicuri de grege porcus* as Horace describes himself in *Epist.* I. 4. 16), but the Epicureans would not have said *permitte divis cetera*, because they believed that the gods were wholly indifferent to mankind.

fuge quaerere. Cf. *fuge suspicari* in II. 4. 22. Another device to avoid a negative imperat. pres. is used in *mitte sectari* (I. 38. 3).

14. **quem...cumque**, *quemcumque dierum*='whatever kind of day.'

15. **appone**, 'set it down to profit,' a metaphor from book-keeping.

16. **puer** with the predicate: 'while you are a boy.'

neque tu choreas, 'nor dances either.' *Tu* merely renews the emphasis, as in *Epp.* I. 2. 63 *hunc frenis, hunc tu compesce catenis.*

18. **morosa**, 'peevish.' *morosus* means literally 'full of *mores*,' i.e. of habits and likes and dislikes: so 'faddish.'

nunc, i.e. while you are young.

18. **areae**, 'piazzas,' open spaces in Rome surrounded by porticoes.

22. **gratus.** The arrangement of the epithets *latentis proditor intimo* and the substs. *puellae risus angulo* suggests that *gratus* is here the predicate: 'is sweet.' (So Kiessling.) Most edd. understand *repetantur* as belonging to this sentence too. Wickham translates 'the tell-tale laugh from the secret corner that betrays the hiding girl.'

angulo, probably the corner of the *vestibulum*, a dark passage leading from the street to the front door.

23. **pignus**, 'forfeit': a bracelet or ring which the young man keeps till the girl redeems it.

24. **male pertinaci**, 'feebly resisting.' For *male* as a quasi-negative cf. *male sanus, male fidus.*

Ode X.

To Mercury, as the Latin representative of the Greek Hermes.

Subject. The prerogatives and attributes of the god and his services to mankind. Porphyrion says the ode is imitated from Alcaeus.

Metre. Sapphic.

1. On the caesura, see *Introd.* p. xxix.

facunde, λόγιος. Cf. Martial VII. 74. 1 *Cyllenes caelique decus, facunde minister.* Mr Page aptly quotes *Acts* 14. 12 'And they called Barnabas Jupiter and Paul Mercury, because he was the chief speaker.'

nepos Atlantis. Hermes (identified with Mercurius) was the son of Zeus and Maia, one of the Pleiades and daughter of Atlas.

2. **cultus,** 'habits,' 'manners.'

recentum, 'new-created.'

3. **voce,** 'language.'

catus, properly 'sharp,' hence 'clever': said by Varro to be a Sabine word. Cf. *egregie cordatus homo, catus Aeliu' Sextus* of Ennius.

decorae, 'graceful,' i.e. *bestowing grace* on athletes (*Introd.* p. xxiv).

4. **palaestrae.** Ovid (*Fasti* V. 667) addresses Mercury as: *Laete lyrae pulsu, nitida quoque laete palaestra, Quo didicit culte lingua favente loqui.* Hermes in Greece was called ἀγώνιος, the god of games.

6. **nuntium.** In Verg. *Aen.* IV. 356 *interpres divom.*

curvae lyrae. The form of lyre invented by Hermes was the *testudo* or χέλυς, a tortoise-shell with strings across the concavity.

7. **callidum...condere,** cf. *Introd.* p. xxiii.

9—12. The order cannot be kept in translation without inversion: "'Twas thou who once in thy babyhood, even while Apollo was bidding thee with awful threats to restore his stolen cows, robbed him of his quiver and set him laughing.'

10. **puerum.** The incident took place on the day of Hermes' birth. Cf. Homer *Hymn. Merc.* 20.

11. **terret** for *terrebat.* The present is preferred with *dum*: as in I. 22. 9: 34. 2.

·**viduus pharetra,** 'deprived of his quiver.' For the abl. cf. IV. 2. 43 *forum litibus orbum.*

14. **dives Priamus.** Priam was going, with rich presents, to Achilles, to ask for Hector's dead body. Hermes guided him through the Greek camp, throwing a spell on the eyes of the Greek warriors so that they should not see him (*Iliad* XXIV.). The wand (*caduceus,* κηρύκειον) with which Hermes cast this spell, was given to him by Apollo when *viduus pharetra risit.*

15. **Thessalos ignis.** The watch-fires of Achilles' men, the Myrmidons, who came from Phthia in Thessaly.

17. **reponis.** *re* often means 'duly,' e.g. *obligatam redde Jovi dapem* (II. 8. 17) where *redde* cannot mean 'pay back': also *sacra refer Cereri* in *Georg.* I. 339. So here *reponis* = 'place them in their *due* abodes of bliss.'

18. **virga aurea,** the same wand with which he safe-guarded Priam. It is spoken of with horror in I. 24. 16.

levem, i.e. shadowy, unsubstantial. So Ovid (*Metam.* X. 14) calls ghosts *leves populos.*

Ode XI.

To Leuconoe, a gay but superstitious lady.

Scheme. Seek not to know, Leuconoe, the day of thy death or of mine. Enjoy the present and think not of to-morrow.

Metre. The Second or Greater Asclepiad (*Introd.* p. xxx), used also in I. 18, IV. 10.

1. **tu,** emphatic: You whom I love and whom I wish to see behaving like a sensible woman.

scire nefas, cf. *nefas videre* in *Epod.* 9. 14, *nec scire fas est omnia* IV. 4. 22.

2. **finem,** 'limit of life.'

nec, not *neu,* because this is not a separate command but consequential to the former one, cf. II. 11. 4 *remittas quaerere nec trepides in usum.*

Babylonios, more generally called *Chaldaeos.* The ancient Chaldaeans were the first astronomers and we inherit from them the division of the circle into 360 degrees and of the hour into 60 minutes. In later times they were noted chiefly as astrologers, who pretended to understand the influence of the stars on human destiny. They had a large following in Rome and under the empire frequent attempts were made to put them down. Horace himself was not free from the superstition which he here decries. In II. 17. 21 he tells Maecenas *utrumque nostrum incredibili modo consentit astrum.*

3. **temptaris,** 'explore,' cf. I. 28. 5.

numeros, 'calculations,' cf. Lucan I. 641 *numerisque moventibus astra*: Juvenal VI. 576 *numeris Thrasylli* (Thrasyllus was a famous astrologer under Tiberius).

ut melius, 'how much better,' cf. *ut gaudet, Epod.* 2. 19.

4. **hiemes,** 'winters' for 'years.' (The figure of 'part for whole' is called *synecdoche.*)

5. **debilitat,** 'tires out.'

oppositis pumicibus, 'against the battered rocks.' The name *pumices* was applied to any *erosa saxa* (Pliny *N. H.* XXXVI. 154).

6. **sapias.** This, with the other punctuation (see Crit. Note), is the apodosis to *seu...seu.* The advice is similar to that in I. 9. 13 sqq.

liques, 'strain,' through a strainer (*colum*) or linen.

spatio brevi, abl. abs. 'the time being short': cf. Livy IV. 41. 12. But some edd. incline to take it as dative = *in breve spatium,* something like Vergil's *it caelo clamor.* (*Introd.* p. xxiv.)

7. **spem longam,** cf. I. 4. 15.

dum loquimur, 'we are wasting time even by talking,' cf. Ovid *Am.* I. 11. 15 *dum loquor, hora fugit.*

fugerit, fut. perf., cf. Lucr. III. 195 *iam fuerit neque post umquam revocare licebit.*

invida, because it grudges us our pleasures.

8. **aetas**, 'time,' as *currit enim ferox aetas* in II. 5. 13.

carpe diem, 'pluck the flower of to-day,' cf. Juvenal IX. 125 *festinat enim decurrere velox Flosculus angustae miseraeque brevissima vitae Portio*.

The sentiment of this Ode is frequently repeated in the *Rubaiyat*, or Quatrains, of Omar Khayyam the astronomer-poet of Persia (flor. A.D. 1100). The following specimen (no. VII. in Fitzgerald's translation) will suffice:

> 'Come, fill the Cup, and in the fire of Spring
> Your Winter-garment of Repentance fling:
> The Bird of Time has but a little way
> To flutter—and the Bird is on the Wing.'

Ode XII.

To Clio. (She was commonly regarded as the muse of History, but Horace does not heed such distinctions. See note on I. 1. 32.)

Scheme. What man or hero or god shall be our theme, Clio? Let us sing them all, Jupiter and the rest, Hercules and the Tyndaridae, Romulus and the other great names of Rome down to Marcellus and Caesar. But Jupiter shall end the song, as he began it.

Metre. Sapphic stanza.

1. On the caesura cf. *Introd.* p. xxix.

lyra vel acri tibia. The lyre should be played by the singer himself: the pipe was played as the accompaniment to a chorus. Clio is thus invoked to inspire either a song or a choral ode. (But see note to I. 1. 32.) The opening is similar to that of Pindar's Second Olympian, ἀναξιφόρμιγγες ὕμνοι, τίνα θεόν, τίν' ἥρωα, τίνα δ' ἄνδρα κελαδήσομεν;

2. **sumis celebrare**, cf. *Introd.* p. xxiii and *Epist.* I. 3. 7 *quis sibi res gestas Augusti scribere sumit?*

3, 4. 'Whose name shall the sportive echo repeat,' cf. I. 20. 6.

5, 6. **Helicon** in Boeotia, *Pindus* in Thessaly, *Haemus* in Thrace, were famous haunts of the Muses.

7. **temere**, 'pell-mell.'

insecutae, sc. *sunt.*

9. **arte materna.** Orpheus was the son of the muse Calliope.

11. **blandum...ducere**, 'alluring.' For the infin. cf. *Introd.* p. xxiii. *blandus* literally means 'coaxing,' 'wheedling.' So *catulorum blanda propago* 'fawning dogs' in Lucr. IV. 999.

auritas, 'listening' lit. 'long-eared,' cf. Plaut. *As.* prol. 4 *face iam nunc tu, praeco, omnem auritum poplum.*

13. **quid prius.** So Verg. *Ecl.* 3. 60 *ab Iove principium.*

parentis, Jupiter, so called again in II. 19. 21.

60 HORACE, ODES I. xii.

15. mundum, 'the heavens,' cf. Verg. *Georg.* I. 5 *vos o clarissima mundi lumina.*

16. horis, 'seasons,' like the Greek ὧραι.

17. unde=*a quo,* cf. I. 28. 28: II. 12. 7 *telluris iuvenes unde.* A similar use of *hinc* in III. 17. 2.

18. secundum (fr. *sequor*)='following close.' Thus *secundus ventus* is 'the wind that follows fast.'

19. proximos, 'next' but not near: as in Verg. *Aen.* V. 320 *proximus huic, longo sed proximus intervallo.*

20. Pallas, identified by Romans with Minerva. Pallas, with the Greeks, was a decidedly bellicose divinity. Aeschylus (*Septem* 119) calls her φιλόμαχον κράτος. Vergil calls her (*Aen.* XI. 483) *armipotens, praeses belli.*

On the punctuation see critical note.

22. virgo, Diana 'queen and huntress,' as Ben Jonson calls her.

25. Alciden, Heracles (Hercules) was the son of Alcmena and grandson of Alceus.

puerosque Ledae. Castor and Pollux were the two sons, Helen and Clytaemnestra the two daughters of Leda. *Puer* is often used by Horace of divine offspring: as I. 19. 2, III. 12. 4.

26. Κάστορά θ' ἱππόδαμον καὶ πὺξ ἀγαθὸν Πολυδεύκεα *Iliad* III. 237, cf. Hor. *Sat.* II. 1. 26 *Castor gaudet equis, ovo prognatus eodem Pugnis.*

superare nobilem, cf. *Introd.* p. xxiii.

27. quorum alba...stella, cf. I. 3. 2 *n.* For *alba* 'clearing,' see I. 7. 15 *n.*

31. ponto. Orelli regards this as dative (cf. *Introd.* p. xxiv).

33—36. The point of the stanza seems to be: 'Who is most god-like? Romulus in his wars, or Numa in his law-giving or Tarquin in his pride or Cato in his death?'

33. quietum...regnum. Numa Pompilius, the peaceful, was regarded as the founder of Roman religious observances.

34. memorem. The construction is: *dubito (utrum) memorem Romulum an q. P. r. etc.*

superbos...fasces. Tarquinius Priscus is said to have introduced the fasces from Etruria. *sup. Tarq. fasces* is a hypallage for *fasces Tarquini superbi.* It is possible that Horace was here thinking not so much of Tarquin as of Brutus, who expelled him.

35. Catonis. M. Porcius Cato, the younger, committed suicide at Utica after the battle of Thapsus (B.C. 46) had given the final overthrow to the senatorial or republican party. His death was regarded as heroic by all good conservatives, cf. II. 1. 24 *cuncta terrarum subacta Praeter atrocem animum Catonis.*

See, however, the critical note.

37—44. The great names of these stanzas are not given in chronological order. M. Atilius Regulus was killed at Carthage B.C. 250:

M. Aemilius Scaurus was consul B.C. 108: L. Aemilius Paulus was killed at Cannae B.C. 216: C. Fabricius Luscinus was consul B.C. 282 : M. Curius Dentatus was consul B.C. 275, and M. Furius Camillus was dictator B.C. 396.

37. **Regulum.** M. Atilius Regulus captured by the Carthaginians B.C. 255: sent to Rome on parole B.C. 250 and killed on his return to Carthage.

Scauros. M. Scaurus and his son. The story, found in Valerius Maximus (v. 8. 4) and other writers, is that the son was among the equites who fled before the Cimbri at the Adige (B.C. 102). The father thereupon sent his son a message so disdainful that the youth committed suicide on receiving it.

38. **Paulum.** L. Aemilius Paulus, consul B.C. 216, refused to leave the field of Cannae and was slain there.

39. **insigni camena,** 'glorious Muse,' i.e. glory-giving, like *nobilis palma* in I. I. 5.

40. **Fabriciumque.** C. Fabricius Luscinus, consul B.C. 282, conqueror of Pyrrhus.

41. **Curium.** M. Curius Dentatus, consul B.C. 275, conquered the South of Italy after the defeat of Pyrrhus. He was a favourite specimen of the ancient Roman simplicity and frugality.

incomptis capillis, cf. *intonsi Catonis* in II. 15. 11. In Horace's time and for long before, all Romans wore their hair short and shaved their faces.

42. **Camillum.** M. Furius Camillus, dictator B.C. 396 and conqueror of Veii.

43. **paupertas,** rather 'frugality' than 'poverty,' which implies want (*egestas*). See I. I. 18 *n*.

apto cum lare, 'with homestead to match.'

45. **crescit...aevo,** 'grows by the unmarked lapse of time' (Wickham): cf. Ovid *Metam.* X. 519 *labitur occulte fallitque volatilis aetas.* Vergil (*Ecl.* 10. 73) compares the growth of love to that of a tree. In Hor. *aevum* often means 'lifetime,' and *occulto aevo* may perhaps mean 'with hidden lifetime' (as in II. 2. 5 *vivet extento Proculeius aevo* means 'P. shall live with extended lifetime'): the sense being that no man knows how long the fame of the Marcelli will go on growing. Or possibly *aevo* is dat. = *in occultum aevum* (cf. *Introd.* p. xxiv).

46. **Marcelli.** The first famous Marcellus was the captor of Syracuse (B.C. 212). The last was the nephew of Augustus and his destined heir, who died in B.C. 23. (The hopes which were founded on him are splendidly described in *Aeneid* VI. 860-886.) The allusion in the text is primarily to the *first* Marcellus, whose fame grows by the exploits of his descendants.

47. **Iulium sidus,** the star of the Julian house, identified by the superstitious with the comet which appeared in B.C. 44 after Caesar's

murder. The 'star' of course is supposed to control the fortunes of Caesar's house.

49. **gentis humanae**, etc. The enumeration began with Jupiter and ends with him. So Aratus says ἐκ Διὸς ἀρχώμεσθα καὶ ἐς Δία λήγετε Μοῖσαι.

51, 52. Cf. Ovid *Metam.* xv. 858 *Iuppiter arces Temperat aetherias et mundi regna triformis: Terra sub Augusto: pater est et rector utèrque.*

53. **seu Parthos**, etc. The point seems to be that Augustus will always acknowledge the supremacy of Jove, even in the hour of his most splendid triumphs.

54. **iusto...triumpho** (with *egerit*, not with *domitos*). *iustus* means 'legitimate,' 'regular,' 'fairly won.' A triumph was *iustus* if the general who claimed it was dictator, consul or praetor, and had himself conducted the battle. The battle must have been with a foreign foe, have decided the campaign and have caused the destruction of 5000 of the enemy.

56. **Seras**, the Chinese. (The English word 'silk' is derived from the adj. *Sericus*.) The Chinese were dimly known to the Romans as having interfered in the affairs of Parthia.

57. **te minor**, cf. III. 6. 5 (*Romane*) *dis te minorem quod geris, imperas.*

59. **parum castis**, 'polluted.'

Ode XIII.

To Lydia. The ode is probably imitated from the Greek and there is no reason to identify this Lydia with her of I. 8 or with any girl of Horace's acquaintance.

Scheme. Lydia, when you speak of Telephus with praise and when I see how he treats you, I burn with jealousy. So rude a boy cannot be a constant lover. How much better is a love that will never be broken by quarrels.

Metre. The Third Asclepiad.

1. **Telephi.** The name is used again for a pretty youth in III. 19. 26 and IV. 11. 21.

2. **cerea**, 'waxen' in colour. Flavius Caper, a very early grammarian, read *lactea*, which many edd. adopt.

4. **difficili**, 'ill-tempered,' 'angry.'

iecur. The liver was supposed to be the seat of the violent passions, whether of jealousy (as here) or of love (as in IV. 1. 12 *si torrere iecur quaeris idoneum*).

8. **quam.** Kiessling connects *quam* with *penitus*, and points out that Horace generally uses *quam* with an adverb (as in II. 13. 21).

9. **uror**, 'I burn' with rage.

10. **turparunt**, 'have stained with bruises.'

immodicae mero, 'rendered violent by wine.'

12. **memorem notam**, 'a scar.'

13, 14. **non...speres**. 'You would not expect.'

perpetuum, 'constant.'

16. **quinta parte**. This is probably to be translated literally. Ibycus (fr. 33) had called honey 'the ninth part of ambrosia,' and another Greek lyrist had called it 'the tenth part of immortality.' Horace therefore, in saying that Venus had steeped Lydia's lips 'with the fifth part of her nectar,' implies that the lips were far sweeter than honey. Orelli, however, and other commentators see in *quinta parte* an allusion to Aristotle's πέμπτη οὐσία (*quinta essentia*) the fifth and highest and purest element: as if *quinta parte* meant 'the fifth ingredient' and so 'the finest essence.'

17. **felices ter**. This substitute for a superlative is common in Greek (as τρισάθλιος, τρίσμακαρ). Verg. (*Aen.* I. 94) has *o terque quaterque beati*. W. von Humboldt suggested that the usage descended from a very early time when people could only count as far as 3 or 4. (See Tylor's *Primitive Culture*, I. p. 265.)

18. **nec**. Observe that *divulsus amor* is really Latin for 'a rupture of their love,' so that only one negative is required. Cf. II. 4. 10 *ademptus Hector* 'the death of Hector' : *Epist.* I. 1. 26 *quod neglectum* 'the neglect of which.'

20. **suprema citius die**. 'Sooner than the day of death (parts them).' Orelli and others think the construction is equivalent to *citius quam suprema die*, 'sooner than on their dying day,' the abl. thus doing double duty, as abl. of time and also of comparison. But this is not good sense, for it is death, and not a rupture of love, that parts them *suprema die*.

Ode XIV.

Scheme. Gain the harbour quickly, O ship. Your hull and your tackle are battered, and your claim to noble origin will not serve you in the storm.

The ode is undoubtedly imitated from one by Alcaeus (see *Introd.* p. xxxviii) which is said to have been an allegorical address to Mytilene, the city and its troubles being typified as a ship and a storm. Quintilian (VIII. 6. 44) quotes this ode of Horace as a specimen of *allegoria* or *inversio* : '*ut* "O navis referent...portum" *totusque ille Horatii locus quo navem pro republica, fluctuum tempestates pro bellis civilibus, portum pro pace atque concordia dicit.*' Dr Leaf has shewn that the last stanza refers to the proposed removal of the capital from Rome to Troy, which is also the subject of *C.* iii. 3. (*J. of Philology* XXIV. p. 283.)

Metre. The Fifth Asclepiad.

2. **fortiter**, 'by a brave effort.'

occupa portum, 'get first to harbour,' before the waves drive you back to sea: cf. *Epist.* I. 6. 32 *cave ne portus occupet alter*. In this sense *occupo* usually has the infin. as in II. 12. 28 and Livy I. 14 *occupant bellum facere*. The corresponding Greek would be φθάνειν with participle.

4. **nudum**, sc. *sit*. For the abl. cf. I. 10. 11 *note*, and *nudus agris, nudus nummis* in *Sat.* II. 3. 184.

6. **gemant** is dependent on *vides*, which (by the figure called *zeugma*) means 'you see' with the first two dependent clauses and 'you perceive' with the third. So *audis* in III. 10. 5 means first 'you hear' and then 'you perceive.' The stock example of *zeugma* (or combination of meanings) in English is Pope's 'See Pan with flocks, with fruits Pomona crowned.'

funibus. In Greek ὑποζώματα, ropes which were passed round a ship, not under the keel but from stem to stern and back again. (See Torr's *Ancient Ships* p. 42). The operation is mentioned in Acts xxvii. 17, where ὑποζωννύντες τὸ πλοῖον is wrongly translated 'undergirding.'

7. **durare**, 'to withstand,' cf. *Aeneid* VIII. 577 *durare laborem*.

carinae, 'the hull-timbers.' It would seem that *carina* is properly not the keel, but the hull of a ship; for the word is applied to the shell of a nut or a mussel.

8. **imperiosius**, 'too masterful.'

10. **di**. Images of protecting gods were placed on the stern of the vessel. Cf. Ovid *Her.* 16. 112 *accipit et pictos puppis adunca deos*, and *Aeneid* X. 171 *aurato fulgebat Apolline puppis*. In many ships of the Mediterranean an image of the Virgin is still carried.

11. **Pontica pinus**. The forests of Pontus furnished much timber for ship-building. Catullus's yacht (the *phaselus* of Cat. 4) was made from Pontic timber.

14. **nil...fidit**, 'the sailor, in the hour of danger, trusts not to gaudy ships' (but to stout ones).

16. **debes ludibrium**, 'unless you have promised to make sport for the winds,' i.e. unless you deliberately wish to court danger. For the expression cf. Greek γέλωτα ὀφλισκάνειν.

cave, 'be careful.' Cf. *Epod.* 6. 11.

17—20. The allegory of a ship battling with a storm is here entirely dropped, perhaps because the Greek poem, which Horace was imitating, went no further. This last stanza is merely advice to the ship of state to avoid dangerous places.

nuper. Horace doubtless refers to the time when he was a political partisan of Brutus (*Introd.* pp. xi, xii).

sollicitum taedium, 'a gnawing discontent.'

18. **desiderium**, 'a yearning' (i.e. object of yearning).

20. **Cycladas**, gov. by *inter* of *interfusa*. Cf. Tac. *Ann.* II. 9 *flumen Visurgis Romanos interfluebat*. The reference here to the proposed rebuilding of Troy forms the connexion between this ode and the next.

Ode XV.

Scheme. When Paris was fleeing across the sea with Helen, Nereus warned him of the fate that awaited him and his native city. The ode is said to be imitated from one by Bacchylides, in which Cassandra utters the prophecies here attributed to Nereus.

Metre. Fourth Asclepiad.

1. **pastor.** Paris was a shepherd in those youthful days when he loved Oenone and was judge in the contest of beauty between the three goddesses.

2. **perfidus hospitam.** The juxtaposition gives emphasis to both words. The crime of Paris was the more base because Helen was his hostess. Cf. III. 3. 26 *famosus hospes.*

3. **ingrato,** 'unwelcome' to the swift winds. Here again the juxtaposition *ingrato celeres* is pointed.

5. **Nereus,** a sea-god, father of the Nereids. He is represented, in vase-paintings, as an old man, sitting on a sea-horse or a Triton, and wielding a trident. Porphyrion seems to have read *Proteus* for *Nereus.*

mala avi, 'with evil omen,' cf. *alite lugubri* in III. 3. 61 and *mala alite* in *Epod.* 10. 1. In Greek ὄρνις and οἰωνός are similarly used.

7. **coniurata.** The reference is commonly taken to be to that oath which Tyndarus required of all the suitors of Helen,—that they would protect the husband whom he should choose. But Vergil mentions another oath taken by the assembled Greek leaders in Aulis. In *Aeneid* IV. 425 Dido says *non ego cum Danais Troianam exscindere gentem Aulide iuravi.*

For the construction cf. Sallust *Cat.* 52 *coniuravere patriam incendere.*

10. **moves,** 'you are stirring.' Cf. *bella moves* in IV. 1. 2.

Dardanae for *Dardaniae.* Cf. *Romula gens* in *Carm. Saec.* 47.

11. **aegida.** The aegis (αἰγίς, 'goat-skin') is in Homer the shield of Zeus, which Pallas sometimes borrows. With later writers, it is the breastplate of Pallas, worn with the Gorgon's head attached to it in front. Cf. *Aeneid* VIII. 354 and 435.

12. **currusque et rabiem.** For the mixture of concrete and abstract cf. *cicatricum et sceleris pudet* in I. 35. 33.

13—20. Cf. *Iliad* III. 54 οὐκ ἄν τοι χραίσμῃ κίθαρις τά τε δῶρ' Ἀφροδίτης ἥ τε κόμη τό τε εἶδος ὅτ' ἐν κονίῃσι μιγείης.

14, 15. **grata...divides.** These words are translated in several different ways, for the meaning of *divides* is not clear and *feminis* may be taken either with *grata* or with *divides.* It seems likely, however, that *grata feminis* are to be taken together, the songs being love-songs, appropriately accompanied by *imbellis cithara (dividere feminis* would mean 'to distribute to women,' by singing first to one, then to another, cf. *dividit oscula* in I. 36. 6). *dividere cithara* is either (1) 'to halve with the lyre,' the song being considered as half air and half accompaniment: or (2) 'to time with the lyre,' i.e. to set to music, as if the lyre marked the divisions of the rhythm: or (3) 'to divide with the lyre,' as if the songs were divided *from one another* by snatches of symphony. The last suggestion seems simplest. The sense then will be: 'you will sing the songs that women love, playing the soft lyre between.'

17. **Cnosii,** Cretan, from Κνωσός, the ancient capital of Crete. The Cretan reed, of which arrows were made, was very strong and had few knots.

18. **celerem sequi Aiacem.** This is Ajax, the son of Oïleus, to be distinguished from the greater Ajax, Telamon's son. The former is called ταχύς, 'swift of foot,' by Homer.

19. **serus,** 'at last.' Cf. Tibullus I. 94 *sera tamen tacitis poena venit pedibus.*

adulteros crines, cf. IV. 9. 13 (*Helene*) *arsit adulteri crines.*

21. **Laertiaden,** Ulysses, son of Laertes.

22. **Nestora,** whose long life is mentioned in II. 9. 13.

respicis, 'do you not bethink you of,' *re-* implying neglected duty, as in I. 2. 36.

24. **Teucer.** See I. 7.

Sthenelus, the charioteer of Diomedes.

26. **Meriones,** a comrade of Idomeneus of Crete.

27. **furit reperire,** cf. *Introd.* p. xxiii.

28. **Tydides,** Diomedes, son of Tydeus. His father was one of the seven champions who fought at the gates of Thebes.

31. **sublimi anhelitu.** *sublimi* doubtless refers to the attitude of the head (whether of the stag or of Paris), 'with panting head up-reared.' *Sublimis* is used in this sense in *Ars Poet.* 457 and elsewhere. In Greek μετάρσιος is almost a technical term for quick, feverish breathing. See Liddell and Scott, s. v. and Euripides *Herc. Fur.* 1093. Orelli and Wickham quote the Greek πνεῦμ' ἔχειν ἄνω which they interpret to mean 'to have the breath high,' i.e. in the mouth but not in the lungs.

33. **iracunda classis,** 'the wrath of Achilles' fleet,' cf. the note on *divulsus amor* in I. 13. 19, 20.

proferet=*differet*, 'will put off.'

34. **Phrygum,** 'the Trojans.'

35. **certas hiemes,** 'a fixed number of years.' Cf. I. 11. 4.

36. **Iliacas.** See Critical Note.

Ode XVI.

To a lady of whom the poet had previously said hard things. It has been suggested that this lady was the Tyndaris who is invited to Horace's farm in the next ode: or the Canidia who is so outrageously abused in *Epodes* 5 and 17 and *Sat.* I. 8. The poem is a palinode or 'recantation' (παλινῳδία) of the kind which Stesichorus wrote when he withdrew his calumnies on Helen of Troy, cf. *Epod.* 17. 42—44. Certainly the attacks on Canidia are written in iambics, and in *Epod.* 17 Horace offers to retract them, but ll. 22—25 seem to show that Horace is not now retracting any poem of his youth, such as the Epodes were. The offence given was recent.

Scheme. Forgive, fair lady, my scandalous lines. I wrote them under the influence of anger, that frightful passion. We inherit it from the savage lion, and much mischief it has caused to the world. When I was young, I gave way to anger, but now I wish to be mild and gentle.

Metre. Alcaic.

1. The lampoon doubtless began *o matre turpi filia turpior.*

2. **quem...cunque,** cf. I. 6. 3 *note.*

modum, 'end.' Cf. III. 15. 2 *nequitiae fige modum tuae.*

3. **pones,** permissive fut. like *laudabunt* in I. 7. 1.

iambis, 'lampoon.' A single poem, written in iambic metre, might be called *ἴαμβοι, iambi.* This metre was first employed by Archilochus in lampoons against Lycambes, who had refused to let the poet marry his daughter. Cf. *Ars Poet.* 79 *Archilochum proprio rabies armavit iambo.* In *Epist.* I. 19. 23 Horace boasts (of his Epodes) *Parios ego primus iambos Ostendi Latio, numeros animosque secutus Archilochi, non res et agentia verba Lycamben.*

3, 4. **flamma...mari,** instr. abl., cf. *agna* and *haedo* in I. 4. 12.

5. **Dindymene,** Cybele, worshipped on Mount Dindymus in Phrygia.

adytis, 'in his inmost shrine,' at Delphi. Here the *adytum* (ἄδυτον, 'unenterable place') enclosed a rent in the ground from which sulphurous fumes ascended. The priestess, stupefied by these, uttered incoherent noises which the priests interpreted as oracular answers.

6. **sacerdotum,** feminine.

incola Pythius, 'he who dwells at Pytho' or Delphi, i.e. Apollo.

7, 8. The construction is: non Liber, non Corybantes, si geminant acuta aera, aeque quatiunt mentem. Cf. II. 17. 13—15.

8. **geminant,** 'clash together': lit. make pairs of.

Corybantes, priests of Cybele.

9. **irae,** personified. *tristes,* 'scowling.'

Noricus, from the iron-mines of Noricum, in the neighbourhood of the Tyrol.

10. **naufragum,** act. 'wrecking.' Cf. *Aeneid* III. 553 *navifragum Scylaceum.*

5—2

12. Iuppiter, 'the sky.' Cf. **I.** 1. 25 *note.*

ruens, 'tumbling.' Cf. *ruit arduus aether* Verg. *Georg.* I. 324.

13—16. The legend is not found in any other author. The construction may be either (1) *fertur P. coactus (esse) addere...et apposuisse,* etc. or (2) *fertur P. (coactus addere...) et apposuisse,* where *et*=etiam: or (3) *fertur P. coactus addere* (for *addidisse*) *et apposuisse,* etc. The third is the most likely: cf. III. 20. 11—13 *posuisse...fertur et recreare,* and Propertius III. 14. 9 *capere arma...fertur nec erubuisse.*

13. principi limo, 'to the original clay,' from which Prom. made the first man and woman.

14. undique, from all other animals.

16. stomacho, not 'anger' as in I. 6. 6, but the actual stomach, as the seat of anger. The English 'spleen' conveys both ideas.

17. Thyesten. It is not known to what form of the Pelopid legend Horace is alluding. In the versions known to us, Atreus perished *exitio gravi* but not Thyestes.

18. urbibus, dat.

ultimae, remotest, and so 'original.'

19. stetere, in prose usually *exstitere*: 'have been.'

20. imprimeretque muris, etc. It was a Roman custom, after destroying the walls of a city, to run a plough over the site of them, as a symbol that the land was henceforth farm-land and not town-land. Carthage was so treated in B.C. 146.

22. compesce mentem. So in *Epist.* I. 2. 63 *ira furor brevis est. animum rege...hunc frenis, hunc tu compesce catena.* Both *mens* and *animus* would seem to mean 'first impulse.'

23. temptavit, 'attacked,' used of a disease, as in Verg. *Georg.* III. 441 *turpis oves temptat scabies.*

24. iambos, doubtless Horace refers to the Epodes, which he himself calls *iambi* (*Epod.* 14. 7) and which were certainly among his earliest works (see *Introd.* p. xii).

celeris iambos, cf. *Ars Poet.* 251 *syllaba longa brevi subiecta vocatur iambus, Pes citus.* Iambics, with their rapid rhythm, are suited to impetuous utterance.

25. mitibus, abl. of *mitia. mutare,* in the sense 'to exchange,' is constructed with an accus. and an instr. abl., the thing given up being in the one case, the thing taken in the other. Here the thing given up is in accus., the thing taken in the abl. But in the next ode, ll. 1 and 2, the opposite constr. is used.

mitibus tristia, 'sours for sweets,' both adjs. having ref. to taste.

26. dum=*dummodo,* 'if only,' as in the famous phrase *oderint dum metuant* (Cic. *de Off.* I. 28. 97), cf. the use of *si* with subj. in the sense 'in the hope that.'

27. recantatis. *recantare* is literally to 'unsing,' to withdraw something already sung. Cf. *reprobo.*

28. animum, sc. *tuum.* Cf. *animum reddere amoribus* in I. 19. 4.

Ode XVII.

To Tyndaris, a young woman not elsewhere named.

Scheme. Faunus himself loves my Sabine farm and protects my flocks. The gods all love me and bless my rustic store. Come, Tyndaris, away from the heat of Rome, and sing and quaff the harmless wine-cup where jealous Cyrus will never find you.

Metre. Alcaic.

1. **velox.** Faunus was supposed to rush about the country in pursuit of the nymphs. Cf. III. 18. 1—4.

Lucretilem, a mountain in the Sabine district, overlooking the valley of the Digentia and Horace's farm there. (See *Introd.* p. xiii.)

2. **mutat Lycaeo**, 'exchanges Lycaeus for Lucretilis,' the opposite constr. from that in the previous ode (see *n.* on l. 25).

Lycaeo, a mountain in the S. W. of Arcadia, the favourite haunt of Pan, whom Horace here identifies with Faunus.

3. **capellis**, dat., cf. Verg. *Ecl.* 7. 47 *solstitium pecori defendite.*

5. **impune**, explained by *deviae*. The goats, though they stray, take no harm.

arbutos. Goats like the leaves of this tree.

7. **olentis...mariti.** The 'rank husband' is the he-goat, *vir gregis ipse caper* (Verg. *Ecl.* 7. 7).

9. **Martialis...lupos.** The epithet is common (*Martius lupus* in *Aeneid* IX. 566). Wolves are fierce and a she-wolf suckled Romulus and Remus, the children of Mars.

haediliae, probably 'kidlings,' a dimin. of *haedus*, like *porciliae* from *porcus*. But the word *haediliae* is not elsewhere found, and most edd. (thinking that goats have been mentioned often enough) print *Haediliae*, as if the wolves came from some wild place called Haedilia.

10. **utcumque**, 'whenever.'

fistula, the 'Pan's pipe' which Faunus plays. He is Lupercus ('wolf-scarer'), and wolves, when they hear his pipe, slink away.

11. **Usticae**, an unknown place.

cubantis, probably 'sloping' (as in Lucr. IV. 517), in contrast to *valles*, but some translate 'low-lying.'

14. **cordi est**, 'is dear.' The expression is common in the later books of the Aeneid and in Livy (usually with *diis* : Roby *L. G.* p. xxxix).

Faunus only protects live stock, but all the gods love Horace and give him abundance of all rural produce.

15. **ad plenum**, 'to the full.' Cf. *ad sanum* = *ad sanitatem* Prop. III. 24. 18.

16. **ruris honorum**, probably dependent on *benigno*. Cf. I. 9. 6 and *vini somnique benigno* in *Sat.* II. 3. 3. But *ruris hon. opulenta* is a possible construction, like *dives artium* in IV. 8. 5 and *dives opum* in Verg. *Georg.* II. 468.

For *honorum* cf. *Sat.* II. 5. 12 *dulcia poma Et quoscumque feret cultus tibi fundus honores.*

cornu (abl. of means), the horn carried by the goddess Fortuna. 'Rich plenty, from a horn liberal of all the glories of the country, shall flow into thy lap till it is full.'

17. **Caniculae.** The Dogstar, also called Sirius, rose in the morning twilight towards the end of July, when the greatest heat began.

18. **fide Teia,** the lyre of Anacreon of Teos, the poet of love and wine.

19. **laborantis in uno,** 'love-sick for the same man,' viz. Ulysses.

20. **vitream,** properly 'glass-green' or 'sea-green.' Circe was a sea-nymph, daughter of an Oceanid, and was tinged with the green of her native element. Cf. Statius *Silvae* I. 3. 85 *ite, deae virides, liquidosque advertite voltus Et vitreum teneris crinem redimite corymbis.* So Thetis, also a sea-goddess, is called *caerula* in *Epod.* 13. 16.

21. **Lesbii.** Lesbian wine was light and therefore *innocens* 'harmless.'

22. **duces,** 'you shall quaff.' *Trahere* is used in the same sense in *Epod.* 14. 4.

Semeleius...Thyoneus, two matronymics, for Semele, the mother of Bacchus, was called Thyone, after her son had made her immortal (II. 19. 28—32).

23. **confundet proelia** seems to be equivalent to *miscebit proelia.* Drunken brawls are fancifully ascribed to a quarrel between Bacchus and Mars. It is possible, however, that *cum Marte* means 'along with Mars,' as if Bacchus sometimes *joined* Mars in provoking quarrels.

25. **suspecta,** 'nor need you fear the jealousy of blustering Cyrus.' *protervus* is applied to winds in I. 26. 2.

male, usually taken with *dispari* ('a very poor match'), on the theory that *male* intensifies a bad epithet but diminishes a good one. But *male* here would go very well with *iniciat.*

26. **incontinentis,** 'frenzied,' unable to restrain themselves: cf. *impotens* in I. 37. 10. The epithet really belongs to Cyrus but is applied to his hands by hypallage: cf. I. 3. 40 *iracunda fulmina.*

28. **crinibus,** dat., cf. *Sat.* I. 10. 49 *haerentem capiti multa cum laude coronam.*

Ode XVIII.

To Varus, probably L. Quintilius Varus, who died B.C. 24 and whose death is deplored in the 24th Ode of this book and possibly also in Vergil's 5th Eclogue. His merits as a critic are mentioned in *Ars Poet.* 428.

Scheme. Varus, plant only vines on your estate at Tibur. Wine is the great dispeller of cares. But it must be used with moderation. Spare me, O Bacchus, thy worst frenzies.

The ode seems to be imitated from one of Alcaeus (*Introd.* p. xxxviii).

Metre. The Second Asclepiad.

1. **Vare**, see above.

severis, a prohibition, like *ne quaesieris* in I. 11. 1 ; *serere* is used of planting trees in Vergil's *Georgics* (e.g. II. 275).

2. **Catill.** The name is properly Catillus, as in *Aeneid* VII. 672. Catillus was the youngest of three brothers, Tiburtus, Coras and Catillus, Arcadians, who founded Tibur. See Verg. loc. cit.

3. **siccis**, 'sober': opp. to *uvidi* in IV. 5. 39 and to *vinolenti* by Cicero (*Acad.* II. 88).

dura, predicatively : 'the god makes every task hard.'

deus, cf. I. 3. 21.

4. **mordaces**, 'gnawing,' cf. *curas edaces* in II. 11. 18.

aliter, without wine-drinking.

5. **crepat**, 'chatters of': generally used of prating, boring talk, but this sense would not suit the next line.

6. **Bacche pater**, also in III. 3. 13. Greeks, who conceived Bacchus as a young man, never call him 'father Bacchus.'

decens, 'pretty,' as in I. 4. 6.

7. **modici**, 'modest,' or 'moderate': cf. *verecundum Bacchum* in I. 27. 3.

transiliat munera, 'should exceed the allowance.'

8. **Centaurea rixa** for *Centaurorum* : cf. *Herculeus labor* in I. 3. 36. At the marriage of Pirithous, king of the Lapithae, with Hippodamia, a drunken Centaur insulted the bride and a terrific combat between the Lapithae and Centaurs ensued. The metopes of the Parthenon and one pediment of the temple of Zeus at Olympia represent groups of the combatants.

9. **debellata**, 'fought out': cf. *decertantem* I. 3. 13 and *deproeliantes* in I. 9. 11.

Sithoniis, the inhabitants of the peninsula of Pallene. The legend here alluded to is unknown.

non levis=*gravis*, 'severe,' 'harsh.'

Euhius, a name of Bacchus derived from the cry εὐοῖ, *evoe*, of his worshippers. So Apollo is called in Greek *Ἰήϊος*.

10. **libidinum**, usually constructed with *fine*, 'by the narrow boundary of their lusts,' i.e. made by their lusts, as if lust narrowed the boundary between right and wrong till it is easily overstepped. But Kiessling proposes to construe *avidi libidinum* together, 'eager for wicked pleasures.' For this sense cf. IV. 12. 8.

11. **candide**, 'fair,' with youthful beauty.

Bassareu, a Thracian name of Bacchus, said to be derived from βασσάρα, the fox-skin worn by Thracian Bacchantes. This is the fourth name applied to Bacchus in this Ode.

non ego te...sub divum rapiam. The passage in effect means that Horace will have nothing to do with orgies. 'I will not shake thee,

fair Bassareus, against thy will, or snatch into the light the secrets that
thou hidest under divers leaves.'

non te quatiam. The reference appears to be to the ceremony of
waking the infant Bacchus, by swinging a cradle containing an effigy of
the god asleep. See the article *vannus* and illustration thereto in
Smith's *Dic. of Antiq.* 3rd ed. Other editors, however, think that *non
te quatiam* means 'I will not shake the thyrsus' (the emblem for the
god himself) and leave *invitum* without comment.

12. **variis obsita frondibus.** The *cista*, a box covered with leaves of
ivy, vine and pine, was carried in Bacchic processions. It contained the
orgia, or mystic emblems, of the god. Among these, snakes seem to
have been the chief. See *Cista Mystica* in Smith's *Dic. of Antiq.*
3rd ed.

13. **sub divum,** 'into daylight.' For *divus* = 'open air' cf. II. 3.
23 and *sub Iove* in I. 1. 25.

tene, 'stop the wild drums.' Horace does not like the noise with
which Bacchanals excited themselves to frenzy.

Berecyntio cornu, a bass horn used in the worship of Bacchus and
of Cybele, who was called Berecynthia from her shrine on Mount Bere-
cynthus in Phrygia.

14. **caecus.** Self-love, personified, is imagined as blind.

15. **plus nimio.** Here *plus* means 'too much,' and *nimio* 'by far,'
cf. *plus paullo* 'too much by a little,' in Terence *Haut.* 2. 1. 8, and
nimio melius 'far better,' in Plautus *Pers.* 1. 3. 31.

gloria, 'vainglory.'

16. **arcanique fides prodiga,** 'Faith that blabs out her secret'
(Wickham): cf. *periura fides* in III. 24. 59. The adjectives here are
essential, not descriptive. It is *mala fides* 'perfidy' that is meant.

Ode XIX.

Scheme. I intended to leave the love of women, but Venus and
wine and idleness have broken my purpose. Venus attacks me with all
her force and forbids me to think of anything but Glycera. Bring me a
turf, slaves, and let me try to mollify the goddess with a sacrifice.

Metre. Third Asclepiad.

1. The line occurs again in a similar connexion in IV. 1. 5.

saeva, 'cruel.'

Cupidines. Usually *Cupido* is identified with *Amor*, the Greek
Ἔρως, but sometimes the two are distinguished. The Greeks also
sometimes distinguished Eros, Anteros, Himeros and Pothos, and these
four, perhaps, are Horace's *Cupidines.*

2. **Semelae puer,** Bacchus, cf. I. 17. 22.

3. **Licentia,** 'idleness,' freedom from restraint.

4. **finitis am.,** 'loves that (I hoped) were done with.'

NOTES. 73

5. **Glycerae.** This name is used again in I. 30. 3, I. 33. 2 and III. 19. 28.

nitor, 'white beauty,' cf. II. 5. 18 *Chloris albo umero nitens*, etc.

7. **protervitas,** 'sauciness.'

8. **lubricus,** 'dangerous.' For *aspici=aspectu* cf. *Introd.* p. xxiii. (N.B. The Latin does not mean 'too dangerous to be looked upon,' but 'very dangerous when it is looked upon.')

9. **tota,** 'with all her force,' cf. Euripides *Hipp.* 443 Κύπρις γὰρ οὐ φορητὸς ἦν πολλὴ ῥυῇ.

10. **Cyprum.** The most famous shrine of Venus was at Paphos.

Scythas. 'To speak of Scythians and Parthians,' means to join in the talk of the town, for these were the great topics of interest (cf. I. 26. 5 and II. 11. 1). The Scythians helped to restore Phraates to the throne of Parthia (II. 2. 17).

11. **versis animosum equis.** Parthian cavalry, while retreating, would shoot arrows at their pursuers, cf. Verg. *Georg.* III. 31 *fidentemque fuga Parthum versisque sagittis.*

12. **quae nihil attinent,** things which do not concern Venus: or humorously, as Mr Page suggests, 'matters of no concern,' as if to a lover politics were unimportant.

13. **vivum caespitem,** a fresh turf, to make an improvised altar, cf. III. 8. 4.

14. **verbenas,** 'green stuff,' any leaves, boughs, etc. that would serve to drape the altar, cf. IV. 11. 6 *ara castis vincta verbenis.*

pueri, 'slaves.' This sudden call to his servants is a favourite device of Horace's. He uses it again in II. 7. 23, II. 11. 18, III. 14. 17, III. 19. 10.

15. **bimi.** See I. 9. 7 *n.* New wine unmixed with water was used in sacrifices, cf. I. 31. 2.

patera, 'saucer.'

16. **mactata hostia.** Animals were certainly offered to the Paphian Aphrodite (Tac. *Hist.* II. 3, Martial IX. 91. 6), but it is doubtful whether they were offered to Venus in Italy. Some edd. consider that the *hostia* here is merely incense and wine. Possibly in III. 23. 18—20 meal and salt, a common substitute for incense, are called *hostia.*

veniet lenior, 'she will come more gently,' no longer *tota ruens.*

Ode XX.

To Maecenas. An invitation to drink wine with the poet.

Scheme. You shall have Sabine wine that I bottled myself at the time of your recovery from illness. The wines of the South are too expensive for me.

Metre. Sapphic.

1. **potabis,** 'you shall drink' (if you care to accept my invitation).

Sabinum, the lightest of Italian wines, said by Galen to be drinkable when between 7 and 15 years old.

modicis cantharis, cups of modest *price* (not size), cf. *Epist*. I. 5. 2 *nec modica cenare times olus omne patella.*

2. Graeca testa. The jar would retain something of the flavour of Greek wine, cf. *Epist*. I. 2. 69 *quo semel est imbuta recens, servabit odorem Testa diu.*

3. levi =*oblevi*, 'sealed up.' Horace himself plastered the cork with pitch (III. 8. 9). But he did not grow the wine himself (as Kiessling points out), for his Sabine farm would not bear grapes. Cf. *Epist*. I. 14. 23 *angulus iste feret piper et tus ocius uva.*

datus...plausus, explained in II. 17. 22. Maecenas, on reappearing in the theatre after a serious illness (B.C. 30), was received with rounds of applause.

in theatro: the theatre of Pompey, built B.C. 55 in the Campus Martius.

5. eques. Maecenas was fond of this title, and had refused to become a senator. See note on I. 1. 1.

paterni fluminis. The Tiber rises in Etruria (*Tuscus alveus* III. 7. 28) and Maecenas was of Etruscan origin (see on I. 1. 1).

For the meaning of *paterni* cf. *paterna terra* in Ovid *Her*. 3. 100.

7. Vaticani montis. The Vatican hill is on the N. side of the Tiber and a considerable distance from the theatre of Pompey. The *i* of *Vaticanus* is long in Martial and Juvenal.

8. imago, 'echo,' as in I. 12. 3.

9. Caecubum, etc. The wines mentioned in this stanza are (with *Setinum* and *Massicum*) the best and most expensive produced in Italy.

Caecubum, grown in the marshes of Amunculae on the coast near Fundi. It is mentioned again in I. 37. 5 and II. 14. 25.

Calenum. From Cales, in Campania, cf. I. 31. 9 and IV. 12. 14.

Falernum. A very strong white wine from the lower slopes of the Mons Massicus in Campania, cf. I. 27. 9 and II. 11. 19.

Formianum, from Formiae near Caieta in Latium, cf. III. 16. 34.

10. Note that Caecuban was the best sort of Formian wine and Calenian of Falernian. Horace has none of these vintages.

11. temperant, *temperare* sometimes means 'to mix' (as wine with water), and most editors so take it here, Falernian vines etc. being said to 'mix the cups' by supplying the wine. But a common meaning of *temperare* is 'to make agreeable,' 'improve'; and that meaning is very suitable here.

Ode XXI.

Scheme. Ye girls, sing the praises of Diana; ye boys, magnify Apollo and Latona too. Diana loves the woods and streams, Apollo loves Tempe and Delos. He will drive away war and famine and pestilence from Rome and Caesar.

This ode may have been written, like the *Carmen Saeculare*, for a special occasion, but no record of such an occasion remains.

Metre. Fifth Asclepiad.

1. **Dianam.** The first syllable is long. It is long also in *Carm. Saec.* 70 but short in *Carm. Saec.* 75.

virgines. The chorus is supposed to consist of girls and boys in equal numbers.

2. **intonsum**, ἀκερσεκόμην. His long hair was a sign of his perpetual youth.

Cynthium. Apollo is so called from Mt Cynthus in Delos, his native place.

3. **Latonam**, the mother of Apollo and Diana.

5. **laetam fluviis**, 'her who delights in streams.' So, in Greek, Artemis is sometimes called ποταμία. *Vos* is 'Ye girls,' opposed to *mares* of l. 10.

nemorum coma, 'the foliage of the groves.' *nemus* apparently is a more open wood than the *silvae* (l. 8), which are dense forests. For the expression cf. *spissae nemorum comae* in IV. 3. 11.

6. **Algido**, a mountain near Tusculum, visible from Rome and near the *lacus Nemorensis* where there was a famous shrine of Diana. It is called *nivalis* in III. 23. 9.

7. **nigris**, referring to the dark colour of pinewoods, while *viridis* in 8 refers to woods of lighter green, such as larches. The woods on Algidus were dark too: see IV. 4. 58.

Erymanthi, a mountain in Arcadia: cf. *nigri colles Arcadiae* in IV. 12. 11.

8. **Gragi**, a mountain in Lycia, the home of Latona.

9. **Tempe**, a valley in Thessaly, between Olympus and Ossa, famous for its beauty, cf. I. 7. 4. Apollo was said to have been purified there after slaying the dragon that guarded Delphi: and there he plucked the laurels for his garland.

10. **Delon.** Legend declared that this was formerly a wandering island, but Zeus fixed it in one place, in order that Leto might there give birth to Apollo and Artemis.

11. **insignemque**, 'and (the god himself) conspicuous with the quiver and his brother's lyre on his shoulder.' *Umerum* is accus. of respect ('as to his shoulder') dependent on *insignem*. The quiver hung at his back, the lyre in front.

12. **fraterna lyra.** Hermes invented the lyre (I. 10. 6) and gave it to Apollo.

13. **hic.** Apollo in his character of ἀλεξίκακος, 'averter of evil,' or ἐπικούριος, 'the helper.'

14. **principe.** See I. 2. 50 *n.*

15. **Persas**, 'the Parthians,' as in I. 2. 22. The Parthians and Britons were enemies, and the remotest enemies, of Rome. It would

seem from III. 5. 3, 4 that Augustus in B.C. 27 announced his intention of conquering both peoples.

16. **aget,** 'will drive away.'

Ode XXII.

To Fuscus Aristius, a very intimate friend of Horace, to whom Epistle I. 10 is addressed. He is said to have been a playwright, and Horace (*Sat.* I. 10. 83) names him among the critics whom he would like to please.

Scheme. The good man needs no protection amidst dangers. For instance, a huge wolf that I met on my farm fled from me though I was unarmed. I was singing the praises of Lalage at the time, and henceforth I will sing them everywhere.

Metre. Sapphic.

1. **integer,** 'spotless,' properly 'untouched.'

vitae, a gen. of respect, said by Roby (*Lat. Gr.* § 1320) to be imitated from the similar use of *animi*, which is really in the locative case. Cf. *Sat.* II. 3. 220 *integer animi.*

sceleris, gen. for abl., imitated from Greek, which has no ablative. Cf. III. 17. 16 *operum solutis.* The abl. is used in *Sat.* II. 3. 213 *purum vitio cor.*

2. **Mauris.** For *Maurus* used adjectivally, cf. II. 6. 3 and *Marsus aper* in I. 1. 28.

5. **Syrtis,** the deserts, not the gulfs, on the coast of Africa.

aestuosas, 'sweltering.' Cf. *aestuosa Calabria* I. 31. 5. Some editors interpret 'boiling' (cf. *barbaras Syrtes ubi Maura semper Aestuat unda* II. 6. 3), but Horace seems to be contemplating a journey on foot.

6. **inhospitalem Caucasum,** repeated in *Epode* I. 11.

8. **Hydaspes,** a river of N. W. India, now called the Jelum. Alexander the Great reached its banks and no doubt the Greek geographers who accompanied him brought back many 'travellers' tales' of the marvels of India.

9. **silva Sabina.** Horace's farm comprised a patch of wood (*silva iugerum paucorum* III. 16. 29) which seems to have been part of a larger forest.

10. **Lalagen.** The name, which means 'prattler,' is used again in II. 5. 19.

11. **terminum,** 'the boundary-stone' of his own farm.

14. **Daunias** (in form a Greek feminine adj., cf. *Ambracias terra* in Ovid) is Apulia, so called from Daunus, an Illyrian king who settled there, cf. III. 30. 11. The Apulians are mentioned as typical soldiers in III. 5. 9 and in II. 1. 34. Horace was born in Apulia and had doubtless seen the wolves and the oak woods of the country.

aesculetis. The *aesculus* is the winter-oak, producing edible acorns.

15. **Iubae tellus.** Numidia, of which Juba was king.

16. **arida nutrix**, an *oxymoron*, or witty contradiction in terms, like *insaniens sapientia* in I. 34. 2.

17. **pigris**, 'stiff,' 'frost-bound.' Cf. Lucretius V. 745 *bruma nives affert pigrumque rigorem.*

19. **quod latus**, condensed for *in eo latere mundi quod.* Cf. Milton's *'what time* the laboured ox...from the furrow came.'

20. **Iuppiter**, 'sky,' as in I. 1. 25.

21. **nimium propinqui**, in the hot South.

22. **domibus negata**, i.e. uninhabitable.

23. **dulce ridentem...dulce loquentem**, imitated from Sappho's ἆδυ φωνεύσας and γελαίσας ἱμερόεν (*Fragm*. 2. 4, 5). For the adverb, cf. *lucidum fulgentes oculos* II. 12. 14, *perfidum ridens* III. 27. 67.

Ode XXIII.

To Chloe, a young woman with whom (according to III. 9) Horace flirted, to the great annoyance of Lydia. But we need not believe that these amours were real, for this ode seems of Greek origin.

Scheme. You avoid me, Chloe, like a fawn that has lost its mother, and starts at the least sound in the bush. But I am no ravening beast, seeking to devour you. Leave your mother's side and look for a mate.

1. **hinnuleo.** The correct spelling is probably *inuleo.*

4. **siluae**, a trisyllable as in *Epod*. 13. 2, and *miluus* in *Epod*. 16. 32.

5. **vepris.** See Critical Note.

6. **rubum**, 'the bramble-bush.'

8. **tremit**, sc. *hinnuleus.*

9. **atqui**, 'and yet.' Cf. III. 5. 49.

10. **Gaetulus.** Gaetulia adjoined Numidia, and was the home of the Nubian lion.

frangere, 'to crunch.' For the infin. cf. *Introd.* p. xxiii.

12. **tempestiva viro**, 'ripe for a husband.' Cf. *Aeneid* VII. 53 *iam matura viro, plenis iam nubilis annis.*

Ode XXIV.

To Vergil, the poet (B.C. 70—19), on the death of Quintilius. This Quintilius is said to have been Quintilius Varus, a native of Cremona, but nothing else is known of him. He is very likely the Varus of I. 18.

Scheme. Who would not weep for Quintilius? He is gone and has not left his peer. You loved him, Vergil, and call upon the gods to give him back, but even Orpheus could not rescue him now. We must bear with patience a loss which we cannot retrieve.

Metre. Fourth Asclepiad.

1. **desiderio** is 'regret' for something lost.

sit, 'need there be.' Cf. such expressions as *quis putet, quis dubitet* (Roby, *Lat. Gr.* § 1538).

2. **capitis**. Cf. *nec te, dulce caput, laesi* Prop. v. 11. 55 and the Greek use of κάρα.

praecipe, 'set a song of mourning.' *praecipere* is to teach by dictation.

3. **Melpomene**, cf. I. 1. 33 *n.*

5. **ergo**, used, as a kind of sigh, to introduce a mournful exclamation. Cf. *Sat.* II. 5. 101 *ergo nunc Dama sodalis Nusquam est!* Ovid *Trist.* III. 2. 1 *ergo erat in fatis Scythiam quoque visere nostris.* The exact English equivalent, in such a position, is 'and.' Cf. Hood's
> '*And is he gone, and is he gone?*'
>   *She cried and wept outright.*

6. **urget**, 'lies heavy on.' Cf. IV. 9. 27 *urgentur...longa nocte.*

7. **incorrupta**, 'incorruptible.' So *invictus* = invincible; *illaudatus* (*Georg.* III. 5) = detestable.

Fides, 'honesty.' Cf. Cic. *de Off.* I. 7. 23 *fundamentum iustitiae est fides, id est dictorum conventorumque constantia et veritas.*

8. **inveniet**, sing. for plural, as in I. 3. 3.

parem, 'his peer,' as in Milton, *Lycidas*, 8, 'For Lycidas is dead, dead ere his prime, Young Lycidas, and hath not left his peer.'

9. **flebilis**, 'bewept': like *illacrimabiles* 'unwept' in IV. 9. 26. This usage is the converse of that in *incorrupta*, supra, l. 6.

11, 12. **tu frustra...deos.** There are several difficulties here:

(1) Most editors take *frustra* with *pius*, but some with *poscis*. The emphatic *tu* favours the former opinion, for the sense appears to be '*you*, such is your grief, actually ask for Quintilius to be restored to life.' Probably *pius* means 'affectionate,' and *frustra pius*, 'with useless fidelity.'

(2) **non ita creditum.** Here *creditum* may mean 'entrusted to the gods,' as if Vergil had once committed Quintilius to their care (cf. I. 3. 5): or 'entrusted to you,' as if the gods had lent Quintilius to Vergil for a time. It might be suggested, again, that *creditum* means 'lendable' (*credibilem* so to say) like *incorrupta* in l. 6.

(3) **ita** is usually interpreted *sub hac condicione*, but the condition is not clear. It may mean 'not entrusted to the gods *to keep*' or 'not entrusted to you to keep for ever,' or 'not entrusted to you, for all your piety,' or 'not entrusted to you, for all your tears.'

Dr Postgate (and apparently Wickham) think *non ita creditum* means 'entrusted to the gods, but not in this plight,' as if Vergil had entrusted his friend to the gods a hale living man and received him back a corpse. (Quintilius evidently died suddenly, perhaps on a journey.)

The following version seems to combine the best of these explanations and to connect the lines with the preceding and succeeding thoughts. 'You, with useless fidelity, ask the gods for Quintilius, whom you entrusted to them, but not in this plight.'

13. **blandius**, cf. I. 12. 11.

14. **moderere**. Cf. Cic. *Tusc.* v. 36. 104 *moderari cantus numerosque.*

15. **sanguis**. Ghosts were supposed to be bloodless. Hence Odysseus, when he wished to make the ghosts speak, allowed them to drink blood (Homer *Od.* XI.).

16. **virga horrida**, 'with his grim wand.' Cf. I. 10. 18.

17. **lenis recludere**. For the infin. cf. *Introd.* p. xxiii : *precibus* is dative after *recludere* and *fata* means the gate of fate. Cf. Propertius v. 11. 2 *panditur ad nullas ianua nigra preces.*

18. **nigro...gregi** = *in nigrum gregem*. Cf. *Introd.* p. xxiv, *Aeneid* IX. 785 *iuvenum primos tot miserit Orco?*

Ode XXV.

To Lydia, a fading beauty.

Scheme. 'Lovers do not attend you so often now with serenades. Soon you will be quite deserted and will rage with jealousy at the younger rivals who have supplanted you.' IV. 13 is an equally disgusting poem on the same subject. III. 15 is less brutal.

Metre. Sapphic.

1. **parcius**, 'more rarely than ever.'

iunctas fenestras, 'closed shutters.' The *fenestrae* are properly the windows themselves, called *bifores* (in Ovid *Pont.* III. 3. 5) because they were closed by a pair of shutters. Windows opening on the street were always placed at some height from the ground and were rarely used in the ground-floor rooms at all.

2. **protervi**, 'obstinate,' 'headstrong.'

3. **amatque**, 'clings to.' Cf. *Aeneid* v. 183 *littus ama* 'hug the shore.'

5. **multum facilis**, 'very easy.' For the adverb, cf. *multum demissus* in *Sat.* I. 3. 57 and *multum celer* in *Sat.* II. 3. 147. For the adj. cf. Juvenal IV. 63 *facili patuerunt cardine valvae.* (Some edd. take *facilis* as nom. sing., comparing Tibullus I. 2. 7 *ianua difficilis*.)

7. **me tuo**, etc. These are the words of the lover, who is cooling his heels in the street. For *tuo* 'your own true-love,' cf. *tuae* in I. 15. 32.

longas...noctes, 'during the long nights.'

9. **invicem** = *vicissim*: 'in your turn.'

moechos, 'paramours.'

10. **solo**, 'deserted.'

levis, 'slighted.' Cf. *elevare*, 'to make light of.'

11. **Thracio vento**, Boreas, which came from Thrace to the Greeks.

magis, 'louder than ever.'

sub interlunia, 'at the change of moons,' i.e. when there is no moon. The ancients believed that this was the stormiest part of the month. For the division of *interlunia*, cf. I. 2. 19 *n.*

14. **matres equorum,** 'mares.' For the periphrasis cf. *olentis uxores mariti* in I. 17. 7.

17. **pubes,** 'young men,' as in II. 8. 17.

hedera...myrto. Take *pulla myrto* together. The sense is 'youth delights in bright-green ivy and dark-green myrtle more than in dry leaves.'

20. **Euro,** see Critical Note. *Eurus* is *hiemis sodalis* just as the Thracian breezes are called *veris comites* in IV. 12. 1.

Ode XXVI.

Scheme. A devotee of the Muses, I have no troubles and care nothing for politics. Come then, dear Muse, and weave a garland for my Lamia. He is worthy of a new, a Lesbian, ode.

It is not known who Lamia was, but III. 17 is addressed to one Aelius Lamia and in I. 36. 7 a Lamia is spoken of as a school-friend of Numida. There was a L. Aelius Lamia who was *praefectus urbi* in A.D. 32 and died in A.D. 33. A scholiast speaks also of an Aelius Lamia who wrote plays.

Metre. Alcaic. This is perhaps Horace's first attempt in this metre (see ll. 6 and 10). It seems to have been written about B.C. 30 (see l. 5).

1. **Musis amicus,** cf. III. 4. 25 *vestris amicum fontibus et choris.*

tristitiam, cf. I. 7. 18.

2. **in mare Creticum,** cf. I. 1. 14 *n.*

tradam portare. The infin. is explanatory. See *Introd.* p. xxiii. Cf. Vergil's *dederatque comam diffundere ventis* (*Aen.* I. 319), 'she gave her hair to the winds for them to scatter.'

3. **quis,** nom. sing. 'who is feared as king.' (Some edd. however take *quis* as dat. plur. sometimes spelt *queis*, 'by whom.') The Romans perhaps were fearing an incursion of northern hordes (cf. I. 19. 10 and III. 8. 18).

5. **Tiridates** became king of Parthia for a short time in succession to Phraates or Prahates IV., who was expelled. It seems that Tiridates raised a rebellion against Phraates about B.C. 33, and after some unsuccessful campaigns fled (B.C. 30) to Octavianus (then passing through Syria after the battle of Actium). From Syria he afterwards made another attempt and managed to expel Phraates in B.C. 27. Phraates, however, recovered the throne early in B.C. 26. There are allusions to the same events in II. 2. 17 and III. 8. 19.

unice, 'alone,' though every one else is full of these topics.

6. securus, 'careless,' 'untroubled.'

integris, 'untouched.' Cf. I. 22. I. The point is the same as in *fidibus novis* l. 10, that Horace is trying a new style of composition. Cf. Lucretius I. 927 *iuvat integros accedere fontes Atque haurire, iuvatque novos decerpere flores Insignemque meo capiti petere inde coronam.*

7. apricos, 'full-blown' by the sunshine.

9. Pimplei, voc. of Pimpleis. The Muses were called Pimpleides, from Pimplea a fountain in Pieria near Mt Olympus.

mei honores, 'the honours that I can give.'

10. fidibus novis...Lesbio plectro. The novelty of the poem consisted only in the adaptation of Alcaics to Latin. Cf. III. 30. 13, where Horace boasts that he was *princeps Aeolium carmen ad Italos deduxisse modos.*

11. sacrare, 'to immortalize.' Cf. Ovid *Pont.* IV. 8. 63 *et modo, Caesar, avum quem virtus addidit astris Sacrarunt aliqua carmina parte tuum.*

Ode XXVII.

Scheme. 'What! fighting over the wine cups! Away with such barbarity! If you wish me to join the party, let some one name his lady-love for a toast—you, for instance, brother of Opuntian Megylla. Come, be not bashful about it. What, is it indeed so bad as that? Poor boy, what magic, what god can rescue you from such a monster!'

The ode is imitated from the Greek, as the allusion to 'Opuntian' Megylla shows.

Metre. Alcaic.

1. in usum laetitiae, 'for the service of gaiety.'

2. Thracum est, 'is worthy of Thracians.' Cf. I. 18. 9 and *Threicia amystis* in I. 36. 14.

3. verecundum. Bacchus is bashful about fighting, but *inverecundus* (*Epod.* II. 13) in talking.

4. prohibete, 'keep clear' as in *Epist.* I. 1. 31 *nodosa corpus prohibere cheragra.*

5. vino et lucernis, dat. cf. *dissidens plebi* in II. 2. 18 and *nepoti discrepet* in *Epist.* II. 2. 194.

Medus acinaces, 'the Persian dirk.' The allusion is doubtless taken from the Greek original of this ode.

6. immane quantum, 'enormously,' is imitated from the Greek ἀμήχανον ὅσον, θαυμάσιον ὅσον. It is really a principal clause meaning 'it is enormous how much'; but the whole clause is treated as one adverb, just as *sunt qui* and *nescio quis* are treated as one pronoun. Livy uses *mirum quantum* and Cicero *nimium quantum* (Roby *Lat. Gr.* § 1647).

impium, 'profane,' as an outrage on Bacchus.

8. cubito...presso, 'with elbow on couch,' i.e. in the position in which the Romans lay at meals.

9. **vultis.** The company is supposed to ask the poet to stay with them and drink his share.

severi = *austeri*, probably what we call 'dry' wine as distinguished from sweet.

10. **Falerni**, cf. I. 20. 9 *n.*

Opuntiae...Megyllae. This name is obviously borrowed from the Greek original. The lady was a Locrian from Opus.

11. **beatus,** 'lucky fellow.'

quo...sagitta, 'of what wound, of what shaft from Love's bow he is languishing.' He is to name the lady as a toast.

13. **cessat voluntas.** Horace turns to the *frater Megyllae.* 'Does your willingness fail?' i.e. are you unwilling?

14. **quae...cumque,** cf. I. 6. 3 *n.*

Venus, 'charmer.' Cf. *melior Venus* in I. 33. 13.

15. **non erubescendis,** 'that need not raise a blush'; lit. not to be blushed for. *erubescere,* which is properly neuter, sometimes takes an accus. as *Aeneid* II. 542 *iura fidemque Supplicis erubuit.* So also *expallescere* has an accus. in *Epist.* I. 3. 10.

adurit, 'scorches' or perhaps humorously 'singes.'

16. **ingenuo...amore.** The epithet 'free-born' belongs to the lady. For the abl. with *peccare* cf. I. 33. 9. For *-que* used 'where the first clause having a negative form, an adversative conjunction would have been more usual, cf. II. 12. 9, II. 20. 4, III. 30. 6' (Wickham, after Dillenburger).

18. **tutis auribus,** ablative of place where. The preposition *in* is usually added, as in *Sat.* II. 6. 46. There seems to be no authority for *deponere* with dat. or with *in* and accus.

The youth here is supposed to whisper in Horace's ear.

19. **laborabas.** Two explanations of the tense have been given. The first and simplest is that *laborabas* means 'you were struggling (when you refused to tell).' The other is that *laborabas* means 'you are struggling, though we did not suspect it': the imperfect being similar to that of ἦν or ἦν ἄρα in Greek, called by Goodwin (*Greek Moods and T.* § 39, p. 13) the imperfect of a 'fact just recognised.' Cf. Sophocles *Phil.* 978 ὅδ᾽ ἦν ἄρα ὁ συλλαβών με 'this, I see now, is the man who seized me.' This explanation gives an excellent sense ('you have been struggling all this time') but the Greek usage is so exceedingly rare (except with ἦν), that it is doubtful if Horace could have borrowed it. See also the note on *erat* in I. 37. 4.

Charybdi, named as a typical voracious monster, cf. Cic. *Philipp.* II. 67 *quae Charybdis tam vorax?* For the abl. cf. *Aquilonibus laborant* in II. 9. 7.

21. **saga, magus, deus,** 'witch, wizard, god,' form a climax.

Thessalis. Thessaly was noted for its witches. See *Epode* 5. 45.

23. **triformi Chimaera,** another voracious monster, with a lion's

head, a goat's body and a serpent's tail. The story is that Bellerophon, riding the winged horse Pegasus, slew the Chimaera by shooting arrows at it from above. Thus Pegasus had a most important share in the exploit.

Ode XXVIII.

Owing to the fact that Archytas is addressed in l. 2 and a sailor in l. 23, it was formerly supposed that this ode was a dialogue between Archytas and the sailor. On this theory, the sailor must say lines 1–6, or 1–16 or 1–20. But if we assign to him ll. 1–6, then *iudice te* etc. in l. 14 makes a Pythagorean philosopher of him: and if we assign to him ll. 1–16 or 1–20, then in l. 23 Archytas asks for burial, though it is clear from l. 3 that he was sufficiently buried already.

But it is now a generally accepted doctrine that the ode is a mono-logue, spoken by the ghost of a drowned man whose body is cast ashore near the tomb of Archytas. The ghost first addresses Archytas and then calls to a passing sailor and asks for burial.

Scheme. Despite your astronomy and soaring philosophy, Archytas, a little dust imprisons you for ever. Well, Pelops died and Tithonus too and Minos and your own master Pythagoras, though he thought that the body alone perished. In truth, soldiers and sailors, young and old, we are all bound to die. I myself was drowned at sea. But ho! sailor! stay a moment and fling some sand on my body. So may a safe voyage and great gains await you. But if you refuse me this little boon, then may the disaster that you deserve overtake you.

Kiessling suggests that this ode is founded on two Greek epitaphs, the first on Archytas, the second on the body of a drowned man whose name was unknown (cf. *Anthologia Pal.* VII. 21 and 265–291): and that Horace has very loosely connected the two together. He points out also that there is some difference in style between the two parts, for after l. 21 the epodes (i.e. the shorter lines) are much more dactylic than before.

1. **maris...mensorem.** No such work is elsewhere attributed to Archytas. There is extant a book of Archimedes, called the ψαμμίτης or 'sand-measurer,' which is devoted to explaining a new system of naming very high numbers, such as would be required in counting the grains of a whole universe of sand. Archytas may have attempted some such problem and also have given an estimate of the size or weight of the earth and sea. His special subject seems to have been mechanics.

2. **cohibent**, 'imprison,' cf. *nec Stygia cohibebor unda* in II. 20. 8.

Archyta. Archytas was a Pythagorean philosopher of Tarentum, about B.C. 460–390. He took a prominent part in politics and was also the greatest mathematician of his day. Plato made his acquaintance about B.C. 393.

3. **pulveris exigui**, 'a narrow grave,' *pulvis* being the mound of earth.

litus Matinum. The place is not known, though Horace alludes to it again in IV. 2. 27 and *Epod.* 16. 27. Horace's evident familiarity with it and the mention of *Venusinae silvae* in l. 26 suggest that it was near Venusia in Apulia; but it is strange that Archytas should have been buried here.

4. **munera,** 'the last gift' to the dead.

5. **temptasse,** 'to have scaled,' a word often used of attacking a walled city.

6. **morituro,** emphatically placed, 'doomed after all to die.'

7. **Pelopis genitor.** Tantalus, who cooked his son Pelops as a feast for the gods.
Tantalus, Tithonus and Minos also have scaled the heavens and become familiar with the gods, but yet they died.

8. **Tithonus,** carried up to Olympus by Aurora.

9. **Minos,** said by Homer (*Od.* XIX. 179) to have been taught, as a child, by Zeus.

10. **Panthoiden.** Pythagoras, who taught the transmigration of souls, used to declare that his own soul had previously belonged to Euphorbus, the son of Panthous, a Trojan hero slain by Menelaus (*Iliad* XVII. 1–60). So Ovid (*Metam.* XV. 160) makes Pythagoras say *ipse ego* (*nam memini*) *Troiani tempore belli Panthoides Euphorbus eram.*

Orco. In Hor. Orcus is a person, cf. II. 18. 30 and 34.

11. **quamvis...concesserat.** For *quamvis* with indic. cf. Roby *Lat. Gr.* § 1627.
Pythagoras died a second time, though it is true—for he claimed knowledge of the Trojan times by taking down his shield—he had not yielded (when he died first) more than his sinews and skin to black death.

clipeo refixo. The scholiast on *Iliad* XVII. relates that Pythagoras once, in the Heraeum at Argos, recognized an old shield as that which he had used at Troy. On turning the shield, the name of Euphorbus was found written inside.

12. **testatus,** probably in the sense of 'bearing witness to,' 'claiming knowledge of.' But it might mean 'avouching,' 'calling as witness.'

14. **iudice te,** abl. abs. like *Teucro duce* in I. 7. 27.

non sordidus auctor, 'no mean authority.' The expression is a good example of *litotes* or *meiosis* (under-statement), for *non sordidus* is intended to mean 'brilliant,' cf. *non levis* 'very severe' in I. 18. 9: *non humilis* 'very haughty' in I. 37. 32.

15. **naturae verique,** almost a hendiadys for 'the truth about nature.' Pythagoras was a *physical* philosopher, concerned with questions about φύσις i.e. the constitution of the world.

una nox, 'unbroken night,' the night which has no dawn.

NOTES. 85

16. **semel**, 'once for all,' as in I. 24. 16.

via leti, cf. *supremum iter* in II. 17. 11.

17. **alios**, 'some,' as if another *alios* followed.

spectacula, 'a show': so *ludus* in I. 2. 37.

18. **avidum**, cf. *avarum mare* in III. 29. 61.

19. **senum ac iuvenum**. Kiessling points out (on I. 12. 15, 16) that Horace uses *ac* where two things together express one universal whole.

20. **caput**, literally, for Proserpine was supposed to clip a lock from the head of every doomed person, as from a victim. Cf. *Aeneid* IV. 698 *nondum illi flavum Proserpina vertice crinem Abstulerat Stygioque caput damnaverat Orco*.

fugit, 'misses': perf. of repeated action (Roby *Lat. Gr.* § 1479) or 'aoristic perfect.' It is, of course, unusual with a negative, cf. *Epist.* I. 2. 47 *non domus aut fundus...deduxit corpore febres* ('never does remove fevers').

21. **devexi Orionis**, cf. *pronus Orion* in III. 27. 18. Orion sets in the morning about the beginning of November, when wintry storms begin to set in.

23. **at tu, nauta**. The ghost suddenly catches sight of a passing ship and calls to the captain.

vagae, 'shifting,' because blown by the winds.

malignus, 'stingy,' cf. *benignus* in I. 9. 6.

parce...dare, cp. *parce...cavere* in III. 8. 26.

24. **capiti inhumato**. For the hiatus cf. *Epod.* 13. 3 *Threicio Aquilone.* Mr Page quotes a very strong instance from Vergil (*Ecl.* 7. 53) *stant et iuniperi et castaneae hirsutae.*

25. **particulam**, 'a small part.'

sic, 'on this condition' (cf. I. 3. 1) viz. that you throw some sand on me.

26. **fluctibus**, dat. *Hesperiis* 'Italian' no doubt refers to the Tyrrhene sea, the sailor travelling westward.

27. **te sospite**, abl. abs. *merces* 'reward.'

28. **unde**, 'from whom,' cf. I. 12. 17 *n.*

defluat, cf. *manabit* in I. 17. 15.

30. **neglegis...te committere**, 'do you think it nothing that you should commit...?' The use of *neglegens* in III. 8. 25 is very similar, cf. also Gk. ἀμελεῖν. Some editors take *te* as abl. with *natis*, 'your children' (cf. note on I. 1. 1), but *neglegis committere* could hardly mean anything but 'do you disdain to commit,' which is the wrong sense.

31. **fraudem**, 'crime.'

forset, 'perhaps,' is said to be syncopated from *fors siet* (=*forsitan*). But *fors* by itself sometimes means 'perhaps,' and Lewis and Short (*s.v.* fors II. A) print *fors et* as two words, with the meaning 'perhaps too.' It is certainly possible that Horace would have ended a line with *et*, but the spelling *forset* is attested by Servius on *Aeneid* II. 139 and XI. 50. Orelli actually contends that '*fors*' here means 'fortune' and is part of the nom. to *maneant*.

32. **debita iura.** *debeo* properly means 'to withhold' (*de-habeo*). As Cicero says (*Planc.* 29. 68), *qui debet, aes retinet alienum.* Here *debita iura* means 'rights unpaid' *to you*, i.e. neglect of your right to burial. All editors, however, take it as meaning 'rights owed *by you*' and regard this as a synonym for 'penalties.'

vices superbae, 'a requital of insolence,' i.e. as Dr Postgate suggests, an insolent requital for your insolence, cf. Prop. I. 13. 10 *multarum miseras exiget una vices.*

33. **non linquar,** sc. *a te,* 'you cannot leave me without incurring vengeance for my prayers (unheard).' *precibus* is the prayer for burial, not the curse, *precibus inultis* abl. abs.

35. **licebit curras,** 'you may go your way.'

36. **ter.** Three handfuls will suffice. *Three* was the ceremonial number, cf. *Aeneid* VI. 229 and 506 *magna Manes ter voce vocavi.*

Ode XXIX.

To Iccius, a student of philosophy, who was intending to join the expedition to Arabia under Aelius Gallus. The expedition, which started in B.C. 24, was a failure. We learn from *Epist.* I. 12. 1, written five years later, that Iccius was then manager of some estates in Sicily (Agrippa's, if the reading is right). Nothing more is known of him.

Scheme. What, Iccius, are you casting a greedy eye on the treasures of Araby and preparing to conquer the Orient? What dusky virgin, what princely boy is to become your slave? Who can deny that rivers may flow upward when you abandon philosophy for war?

Metre. Alcaic.

1. **beatis,** 'rich. The epithet is properly applied to persons, as in II. 4. 13.

Arabum. Owing to the great cost of spices, pearls, ivory and other oriental products which reached Europe by way of the Red Sea, exaggerated ideas prevailed in Rome about the wealth of Arabia, cf. II. 12. 24 and III. 24. 1 *intactis opulentior thesauris Arabum.*

2. **gazis,** a Persian word.

3. **Sabaeae,** 'Sheba' in the S. of Arabia.

4. **Medo.** There is a kind of climax here, as if the expedition were likely to go further and further into Asia, and to win the long-desired victory over the Parthians. Horace of course is 'chaffing' his friend.

5. **quae virginum barbara.** Wickham compares *Graia victorum manus* in *Epod.* 10. 13.

6. **sponso necato.** She was betrothed to some barbarian prince, cf. III. 2. 8–10.

7. **ex aula.** The boy too is a princeling. Horace playfully imagines Iccius as another Alexander the Great.

8. **ad cyathum.** The *cyathus* was a ladle or dipping-cup, and the duty of the boy would be to ladle out wine (watered) from the *crater* or mixing-bowl.

9. **doctus...paterno.** The boy belongs to a race of noble warriors.

Sericas, 'Chinese' (cf. I. 12. 56 *n.*), is a continuation of the banter about the extraordinary boldness of this expedition.

10. **arduis montibus,** usually regarded as dat. = *in arduos montes,* cf. *Introd.* p. xxiv. But it might be abl. of the place where, for the upward course of the rivers is sufficiently indicated by *re-* in *relabi* after *pronos.*

13. **nobilis Panaeti.** Cf. *Epist.* I. 19. 13 *nobilium scriptorum.* Panaetius of Rhodes was a Stoic philosopher and friend of the younger Africanus and Laelius. He wrote a work on Duty (περὶ τοῦ καθήκοντος) which is substantially reproduced in the first two books of Cicero's *De Officiis.*

14. **Socraticam domum,** 'the Socratic school,' i.e. the school of philosophy founded by Socrates (B.C. 469–399). The chief representative of the school is Plato, but Xenophon the historian, Eucleides of Megara, Antisthenes of Athens and Aristippus of Cyrene were all pupils of Socrates.

15. **mutare...tendis,** cf. III. 4. 51. *Epist.* I. 19. 16 *tenditque disertus haberi.* For the construction of *mutare* cf. I. 16. 25 *n.*

loricis Hiberis. The Spaniards were famous for steel and these *loricae* seem to be cuirasses of chain-mail.

Ode XXX.

To Venus.

Metre. Sapphic.

1. **Cnidi,** a promontory in Caria, the S.W. corner of Asia Minor.

Paphi, in Cyprus, cf. I. 3. 1 and I. 19. 9.

2. **sperne,** 'desert,' cf. III. 2. 24.

3. **Glycerae,** cf. I. 19.

4. **aedem,** 'temple.' Either Glycera's whole house is converted into a temple by the presence of the goddess, or else we must suppose that Glycera had just made a little shrine to Venus and had asked Horace to write a little ode for the dedication, cf. IV. 1. 19, 20.

5. **solutis zonis** (abl. abs.), 'loosely girt' and therefore ready for the dance, cf. I. 4. 6.

6. **properentque.** For the order of the words cf. II. 17. 16 *Iustitiae placitumque Parcis,* II. 19. 28 *pacis eras mediusque belli.* Also II. 7. 24 and *Carm. Saec.* 22.

8. **Mercuriusque.** The worship of Hermes, in Greece, was frequently associated with that of Aphrodite. Here perhaps Mercury is introduced as *facundus* (I. 10. 1) to lead the conversation.

Ode XXXI.

To Apollo, on the completion of his new temple on the Palatine. This temple, promised by Octavian after the battle of Mylae B.C. 36, was eight years in building and was dedicated with great pomp on Oct. 24, B.C. 28. Attached to it there was a large public library and a collection of fine sculptures.

Scheme. What does the poet ask of Apollo in his new shrine? Not lands or flocks or gold or other kinds of wealth, such as a merchant wins by braving the sea. A humble fare suffices for me, but grant me, O Apollo, content, good health, a sound mind and an honourable old age, solaced by poetry.

Metre. Alcaic.

1. **dedicatum.** *dedicare deum* meant to dedicate a statue of the god, cf. Ovid, *Fast.* VI. 637 *te quoque magnifica, Concordia, dedicat aede.* The statue of Apollo in the Palatine temple was a famous work of Scopas (*flor. circa* B.C. 360) brought from Greece.

2. **novum liquorem,** cf. I. 19. 15 *n.*

3. **opimae,** 'fat,' 'rich': cf. *Larissae campus opimae* I. 7. 11.

4. **segetes,** 'corn lands,' for which Sardinia was renowned.

5. **grata** is usually explained as 'pleasant' to look upon. Kiessling, however, suggests that *feraces* and *grata* are both predicative: 'not that my cornlands in Sardinia may be fertile, not that my flocks in sultry Calabria may be grateful' (i.e. may repay my care).

Calabriae. Calabria was in ancient times, in spite of its drought (hence *aestuosae* cf. I. 22. 3), a famous pasture country, noted especially for a breed of long-woolled sheep. These perhaps are the *armenta* of l. 6, cf. *dulce pellitis ovibus Galaesi flumen* in II. 6. 10 and also *Epod.* I. 27.

7. **Liris,** a river of Campania, flowing through the best vine-districts.

9. **premant,** 'let them prune.' For *premere* in the sense of 'check,' 'cut back' cf. *Georg.* I. 156 *ruris opaci Falce premes umbram.*

Calena. Cf. I. 20. 9 *n.* The epithet belongs more strictly to *vitem* and many editors read *Calenam* here, as Porphyrion the scholiast (*Introd.* p. xxxvi) did. Compare, however, III. 6. 38 *Sabellis docta ligonibus Versare glaebas.*

10. **vitem** is object both to *premant* and *dedit.*

11. **culullis** (also spelt *culillis*). These were properly cups used by the Pontifex and the Vestals in pouring libations. They seem to have been large, though the word is a diminutive, somehow connected with Greek κύλιξ 'a cup.'

12. **Syra merce.** Spikenard (cf. II. 11. 16 *Assyrio nardo* and also II. 7. 8, III. 1. 44) and rich carpets and hangings were imported from Syria through Tyre (III. 29. 60). For *Syra* cf. *Marsus aper* I. 1. 28.

reparata is usually interpreted 'procured in exchange.' *Syra merce* is thus abl. instr. (as with *mutare* I. 16. 26 *n.*). This use of *reparare* is certainly very rare, and Bentley denied it altogether. He thought that *reparata Syra merce* meant 'mixed with spikenard,' according to the practice of wealthy Romans.

The merchant, who goes three or four times a year to the *aequor Atlanticum* (l. 14), would not bring Syrian merchandise thence. If *reparata* means 'procured,' we must suppose that the merchant, being rich, brought choice unguents to the dinner-party as his contribution. It was usual, in Rome, to bring such presents to the host (IV. 12. 14, 16).

13. **dis carus ipsis**, 'the favourite' (not of fortune only, but) of the gods themselves.

16. **leves**, 'easily digestible.' Cf. *Epod.* 2. 58 *gravi malvae salubres corpori*.

17. **frui paratis**, 'to enjoy what I have gained.'

valido, 'sound in body' as well as *integra cum mente*. But see next note.

18. **et**. See critical note. Those editors (as Wickham) who read *at* interpret *valido* as 'while I am young and strong' and make *nec turpem senectam* etc. the complement to *et valido*: so that the prayer is *dones mihi et valido frui paratis* (*at integra cum mente*) *nec* (= et non) *turpem senectam degere* etc. But this does not give a good sense, for a man wishes *frui paratis* when he is old even more than when he is young, nor does anybody fear that his mind will decay while he is *validus*. The text is far better. 'Grant to me, son of Leto, that I may enjoy what I have both with good health and with sound mind, and that I may not pass my old age disgusting to everybody and without the solace of poetry.' Horace wishes to be hale and hearty to the end.

With *valido* one would like to supply a present participle of *esse*, *valido ὄντι* so to say.

Ode XXXII.

To his lyre.

Scheme. They ask me for an ode. If the songs that we have sung together have claims to immortality, try now, my lyre, a Latin strain, such as the Greek to which thou wert tuned by Alcaeus, the patriot, the sailor, yet the poet of love. Glory of Phoebus, darling of the gods, solace of toil, help me when I call thee!

Metre. Sapphic.

1. **poscimur**. See critical note. Editors conjecture that Horace had been asked by Augustus or Maecenas to compose some more serious and lofty odes, such as III. 1–6. But the conjecture is quite unwarranted by the poem. In ll. 8–12 Horace lays stress on the fact that Alcaeus wrote of love and in ll. 13–16 he lays stress on the gentle charm of the lyre. The inference is that he was asked now to write a love-poem in Alcaics. The use of *vacui* supports this.

siquid. A humble manner of suggesting that the poet had received similar favours before. Cf. *Carm. Saec.* 37 *Roma si vestrum opus est* etc.: Verg. *Georg.* I. 17 *tua si tibi Maenala curae, Adsis, O Tegeaee, favens.*

vacui, not 'in an idle hour,' but 'fancy-free' as in I. 6. 19. The allusion is to such poems as I. 26 or 27.

2. **lusimus,** with acc. cf. IV. 9. 9 *siquid olim lusit Anacreon.*

quod...pluris. Kiessling, to some extent following Bentley, takes *Latinum carmen* to be the antecedent of *quod*, 'a Latin ode that may live.' But apart from the ungainliness of such Latin, the adjuration loses force. 'Sing an immortal song, for we have sung together before' is not so effective as 'Sing a song, for we have sung immortal songs together ere now.'

3. **dic.** Cf. I. 17. 19 and III. 4. 1.

4. **barbite.** This word, which is pure Greek, and *Lesbio* in l. 5 throw emphasis, by contrast, on *Latinum*.

5. **Lesbio civi,** Alcaeus, who is called *civis* perhaps to indicate his political activity against the tyrants Myrsilus and Pittacus.

modulate is passive. Cf. I. 1. 25 *n.*

6. **ferox bello,** 'though spirited in war.' Cf. II. 13. 26 and IV. 9. 7.

7. **sive,** 'or if,' as in I. 6. 19.

religarat, 'had tied up' as in I. 5. 4. N.B. *religare* sometimes means 'to untie.'

udo, wet with the same storm that tossed the ship.

9. **illi...haerentem,** 'cleaving to her side' as in *Aeneid* X. 780 *missus ab Argis haeserat Evandro.*

11. **nigris...decorum.** Cf. *Ars Poet.* 37 *spectandum nigris oculis nigroque capillo.*

13. **decus Phoebi.** Cf. I. 21. 12.

15. **mihi...vocanti.** These words seem to mean 'be gracious to me always when I duly call thee.'

cumque. In previous odes (see I. 6. 3 *n.*) we have had many examples of tmesis in *quicumque* and it is possible that Horace regarded *cumque* as a separate word related to *quisque* as *cum* is to *qui*. It would mean 'ever,' i.e. 'always' or 'at any time.' No doubt *cumque* was at one time a separate word (like *quandoque*), but it is not found by itself elsewhere.

salve, which is ordinarily a formula of greeting or farewell, is sometimes rather a formula of worship. In this use, it may be a version of the Greek ἵληθι 'be gracious' (as Dr H. Jackson suggests). If so, then *salve mihi rite vocanti* is a legitimate expression: cf. the Publican's prayer in Luke xviii. 13 ὁ θεὸς ἱλάσθητί μοι τῷ ἁμαρτωλῷ. The nearest parallels are Verg. *Georg.* II. 173 and *Aen.* VIII. 301, where a hymn to Hercules ends with *Salve, vera Iovis proles, decus addite divis Et nos et tua dexter adi pede sacra secundo.*

Ode XXXIII.

To Albius, perhaps Tibullus the poet (died B.C. 18). The cruel Glycera is, however, not mentioned by that name in any extant poem of Tibullus. She is supposed to be identical with the lady called Nemesis in Tib. II. 3. 4. The Albius addressed in *Epist.* I. 4 was obviously a rich man, whereas the poet Tibullus was poor. The identification is therefore far from certain.

Scheme. Grieve no more, Albius, for the cruelty of Glycera and leave off writing elegies on her perfidy. Lycoris loves Cyrus, and Cyrus loves Pholoe, who loathes him. Such is the sport of Venus. I was a victim to it myself at one time.

Metre. Fourth Asclepiad.

1. **ne doleas.** Editors have generally regarded this as a final clause:—'In order that you may not grieve, I will tell you about Lycoris and Cyrus.' The reason given (also at II. 1. 37 and IV. 9. 1) is that grammarians do not admit this form of prohibition, when addressed to a particular person, but require *ne* with perf. subj. or *noli* with infin. Thus Roby says (§ 1600 *n.*) 'In prohibitions *to a definite person*, the present subjunctive active is found occasionally in comic poets: once in Horace (*Sat.* II. 3. 88), once only in Cicero,' etc. But if the statistics collected by Prof. H. C. Elmer (in *American Journ. of Philology* XV. 133) can be trusted, the rule is quite misconceived. In classical Latin prose (Cicero to Livy) a general prohibition of the form *ne facias* is exceedingly rare. In personal prohibitions, *noli facere* or *cave facias* or *cave feceris* are the commonest forms: *ne facias* not at all uncommon and *ne feceris* very uncommon (only occurring seven times, all in Cicero). The difference (according to Prof. Elmer) between *ne feceris* and *ne facias* is that the former is peremptory and passionate, the latter mild and polite.

If this is the practice of the prose-writers, there need be no hesitation about constructing *ne doleas* here as a prohibition: 'do not grieve.'

plus nimio, with *doleas.* Cf. I. 18. 15 *n.*

2. **Glycerae.** See on I. 19.

miserabilis, 'piteous.'

3. **decantes.** *decantare* is 'to sing to the very end' and so 'to sing tediously.'

elegos, 'elegiacs,' i.e. poems in elegiac metre, as *iambi* (I. 16. 2) are poems in iambic metre.

cur, 'asking why.' Cf. *Epist.* I. 8. 10 *irascar amicis Cur me funesto properent arcere veterno.*

4. **praeniteat,** 'outshines you' in Glycera's eyes.

laesa fide, abl. abs.

5. **tenui fronte,** 'with low forehead.' The Romans liked the hair so arranged that only a narrow space of forehead was seen between the hair and the eyebrows. Cf. *Epist.* I. 7. 26 *nigros angusta fronte capillos.*

Lycorida. The name may be borrowed from the elegies of Gallus. See Verg. *Ecl.* x. 2.

6. **Cyri.** This name has been used in I. 17. 25.

asperam, 'unfriendly.' She 'bristles up' at him. Cf. *monitoribus asper* in *Ars Poet.* 163 and *tigris aspera* I. 23. 9.

7. **declinat,** 'turns away' from Lycoris.

Pholoen. The name occurs also in one of Tibullus' poems (I. 8). Horace uses it again in II. 5. 17 and III. 15. 7.

Apulis lupis. Cf. I. 22. 18.

8. **iungentur capreae lupis.** Cf. Verg. *Ecl.* VIII. 26 *Mopso Nisa datur : quid non speremus amantes ? Iungentur iam grypes equis.*

9. **turpi adultero,** 'an ugly lover.' For the abl. cf. *ingenuo amore peccas* in I. 27. 17. For *adulter* cf. *moechos* in I. 25. 9 and also I. 36. 18.

10. **sic visum Veneri,** 'such is the will of Venus.' Cf. *dis aliter visum* in *Aeneid* II. 428.

11. **iuga aenea.** We should say 'iron yoke.' The expression occurs again in III. 9. 18.

13. **melior Venus,** 'a nobler love.' Cf. I. 27. 14 *n.*

15. **acrior,** 'more passionate' (Wickham).

libertina. Bentley quotes a great number of inscriptions in which Myrtale appears as the name of a freedwoman.

Hadriae. Cf. I. 3. 15 and III. 9. 22.

16. **curvantis,** 'hollowing out the round bays of Calabria.' *curvare* is 'to make curved': so Lucan VIII. 177 *Scythiae curvantem litora pontum.* (Some interpret 'curling the Calabrian waves,' but *fretis* has already called up the image of waves.) But here *curvare sinus* means 'to make round bays,' for the sea makes the bays and rounds them too. Cf. *confundere proelia* in I. 17. 23 'to make confused battles,' and *consociare umbram* in II. 3. 10 'to make a joint shade.'

Ode XXXIV.

Scheme. I, whose foolish philosophy made me an infrequent worshipper of the gods, am now obliged to change my opinions. For I heard Jupiter thunder from a clear sky with such a clap that all the world was shaken. The gods, I confess it now, do interfere in the affairs of men, to exalt the lowly and bring down the proud.

Metre. Alcaic.

1. **parcus cultor,** 'a niggardly worshipper,' because he offered scanty sacrifices.

2. **insanientis sapientiae consultus,** 'professor of a senseless philosophy.' *consultus* is 'a person who is consulted,' i.e. a professor. For the gen. cf. *iuris consultus* (Roby *L. G.* § 1316 and 1319). *insaniens philosophia* is an oxymoron: cf. I. 18. 16 *n.* The philosophy in question is that of Epicurus, who maintained that the gods did not

concern themselves with human affairs or with the control of the universe.

3. **erro,** I wander from the right way.

4. **iterare cursus relictos** is not the same thing as *vela dare retrorsum.* Horace sails back again to the point he started from and thence *iterat cursus relictos,* i.e. begins again the course he had abandoned. In other words, he falls back on the beliefs of his childhood. *iterare* is to do a thing twice by beginning it again, not to do it backwards: so *iterare pugnam, proelium, verba, dicta* etc.

5. **Diespiter** (again in III. 2. 29) is an older form of the same name as *Iuppiter* (and Ζεὺς πατήρ), the original *diēus* being differently altered in the two names. (*Iuppiter* is said to be voc. turned nom.)

7. **plerumque** has the emphatic position, but in translation the emphasis falls on *nubila* and *per purum,* 'Jupiter who usually rends the *clouds,* drove his thundering horses and swift car through the *clear sky.*'

per purum. It happens that Lucretius, in his poem *De Rerum Natura,* which is an exposition of Epicurean doctrines, asks why there is never thunder in a clear sky. (*Denique cur nunquam caelo iacit undique puro Iuppiter in terras fulmen sonitusque profundit?* Lucr. VI. 400.) The inference which Lucretius draws is that, as it never thunders when there are no clouds, the clouds, and not Jupiter, are the cause of the thunder.

9. **quo,** sc. *curru.*

bruta, 'heavy,' 'motionless' (*iners terra* in III. 4. 45) in contrast to *vaga flumina.*

10. **Taenarum,** now Cape Matapan, the southernmost point of the Peloponnesus. There is a cave here which was supposed to be one of the entrances to Avernus.

11. **Atlanteus finis,** 'the boundary that Atlas makes.'

12. **valet ima** etc. Here Horace makes profession of his new faith. *valet* is emphatic: 'Jupiter *can* overturn the world.'

13. **mutare.** See I. 16. 27 *n.*

14. **apicem,** 'the tiara,' as a symbol of royalty. Cf. III. 21. 20. The *apex* here in view is the same as the *diadema* of II. 2. 21, a cap, encircled by a blue and white band, worn by Persian kings. (See Smith's *Dict. of Antiq.* 2nd ed. *s. vv. Apex, Diadema, Tiara.*)

15. **stridore,** 'with shrilly-whirring wings.' So Fortune *celeres quatit pennas* III. 29. 53. Cf. *Aeneid* I. 397 *stridentibus alis.*

16. **sustulit...posuisse.** The perfect seems to indicate the suddenness of the two actions. So Verg. *Georg.* I. 330 *terra tremit: fugere ferae: Georg.* III. 104 *campum Corripuere ruuntque, effusi carcere currus* (also in *Aeneid* V. 145). Most editors, however, call *sustulit* here an 'aoristic perfect,' indicating an action often repeated, and explain *posuisse* as 'to place and keep it placed.'

Ode XXXV.

To Fortune.

Scheme. Goddess of Antium, ruler of the lives of mortals, the poor rustic, the sailor, the barbarian, all peoples, cities and kings worship thee. Necessity marches before thee: Hope and Faith attend thee and follow thee, when false friends flee. Preserve our Caesar who is going to Britain and our army that is going to Arabia. We are ashamed of our civil strifes: sharpen thou our swords against the foreign foe.

The word *fortuna* in Latin (like *nature* or indeed *fortune* in English) is used in several senses which Horace here confuses. It means (1) the force that controls events: (2) events themselves, and (3) the condition produced by events, namely, the prosperity or adversity of a nation, family or person. In each of these aspects *fortuna* may be personified, and Horace uses all three personifications. In ll. 1–16, Fortuna is the goddess who rules human life: in 17–20, she is life itself or history, preceded by Necessity: in 21–28 she is *fortuna domus*, the prosperity of a noble family: and in 29–40 she is the *fortuna populi Romani*, the prosperity of the Roman people. These personifications, however, are not imagined distinctly by Horace and he in places confuses his imagery.

Metre. Alcaic.

1. **gratum Antium**, 'your dear Antium' (cf. III. 26. 9). Antium is a promontory in the Volscian territory, where there was a famous temple and oracle of two Fortunae. They are supposed to have been Prospera and Adversa, but this is a mere conjecture from the fact that one is represented wearing a helmet and the other wearing a fillet. Fortuna singly is usually represented with a cornucopiae and a rudder.

2. **praesens**, 'ready' and so 'able.' Cf. Psalms xlvi. 1 'a very present help in trouble.' So *praesentissimum remedium* 'a most efficacious remedy.'

3. **mortale corpus**, contemptuously 'a mere unit of mortality.'

4. **funeribus**, abl., *vertere* being equivalent to *mutare*. Cf. I. 16. 26 *n.* and *vertere seria ludo* in *Ars Poet.* 226.

5. **pauper**, the poor husbandman is contrasted with the rich merchant (cf. I. 31. 10).

6. **ruris** probably goes with *dominam*.

7. **Bithyna.** Cf. *Pontica pinus* in I. 14. 11. **lacessit**, 'tempts.'

8. **Carpathium pelagus**, so called from the island Carpathus, between Rhodes and Crete.

9. **asper**, perhaps 'fierce' as *tigris aspera* in I. 23. 9. Wickham suggests that the Dacian, who stands at bay, is contrasted with the Scythian, who eludes pursuit. But *asper* may mean 'unkempt' and contrast the savage Dacian and Scythian with the civilised *urbesque gentesque et Latium ferox.*

A verb must be supplied for all these nominatives either from *ambit* in 5 or *metuunt* in 12.

11. **regumque matres.** Cf. III. 2. 7.

12. **purpurei,** 'in the purple,' i.e. in all their state.

13. **iniurioso,** 'contemptuous,' *Epod.* 17. 34.

14. **stantem columnam,** in Greek ὀρθοστάτην. *columna* means 'prop,' 'support,' like *columen* in II. 17. 4. When this is overthrown, the house falls. Cf. Eur. *H. F.* 980 and 1007.

15. **ad arma...ad arma.** This is the cry of the *populus frequens.* Cf. Ovid, *Met.* XII. 241 *certatimque omnes uno ore 'arma, arma' loquuntur.*

cessantis, 'the laggards.'

17—20. The symbolism of this stanza is very obscure. Probably the nails and clamps, which Necessitas or Doom carries, are mere symbols of fixity and Doom carries them because doom and fixity are inseparable. (In III. 24. 6 however Doom is represented as using the nails in some way.) If this view be correct, it is still not clear why Doom precedes Fortune. Probably Fortuna, in this stanza, is life in general, the condition of mankind (cf. Cicero *Off.* I. 13. 41 *condicio et fortuna servorum*).

18. **clavos trabalis,** 'nails for fastening timber.'

cuneos, 'wedge-shaped nails.'

19. **aena,** as we might say 'in her iron hand.' Cf. *aena iuga* in I. 33. 11.

severus, 'grim.' Cf. *amnis severus Cocyti* in Verg. *Georg.* III. 37.

20. **uncus,** 'clamp,' fixed in its sockets by molten lead.

21—28. The Fortune here addressed is the Luck of noble houses, which is cheerful when they are prosperous, sad when they are in distress. (Cf. IV. 4. 70 *occidit Spes omnis et fortuna nostri Nominis.*) This is *fortuna* in the sense of 'what happens.' But the insertion of *inimica* in l. 28 spoils the conception, for the Luck of a house cannot be hostile to it.

21. **Spes...Fides.** Hope and Faith were often worshipped in conjunction with Fortuna, but Horace uses *Fides* in the sense of 'loyalty. *rara* means 'seldom seen.'

albo velata panno. It is usually supposed that Fides is imagined with her right hand wrapped in a white napkin. Livy (I. 21) says that the flamen who sacrificed to Fides had his right hand thus wrapped, to symbolize both the secrecy of Faith and the purity of the pledge of the right hand. But in *Epist.* I. 17. 25 Horace speaks of the philosopher *quem duplici panno patientia velat,* referring to his ample cloak, and this is probably the meaning of *pannus* here. The large white cloak symbolizes secrecy and purity as well as the white napkin.

nec comitem abnegat, i.e. *se abnegat,* 'and does not refuse herself as a companion to thee.' So Ovid, *A. A.* 1. 127 *si qua repugnarat nimium comitemque negarat.*

23. **mutata veste,** 'in changed garb,' i.e. in the garb of mourning. Cf. *Epod.* 9. 28 *punico Lugubre mutavit sagum.*

24. potentis domos. The great families of Rome had their own Fortuna, as Fortuna Torquatiana, Tulliana, Caesariana.

inimica. This word, as was pointed out above, disturbs the conception, for the Fortune of a house is practically the *history* of the house, and cannot be hostile to it. She suffers what the house suffers. Cf. *Epist.* II. I. 191 *trahitur manibus regum fortuna retortis.*

26. cadis...siccatis, abl. abs. Cf. the Greek proverb ξεῖ χύτρα, ξῇ φιλία, and the English one 'when poverty comes in at the door, love flies out at the window.'

28. ferre iugum pariter dolosi, 'dishonest in bearing the yoke equally,' i.e. not true yoke-fellows, a metaphor from a pair of cattle that do not work equally hard together.

29—40. The Fortuna of these stanzas seems to be the Fortuna Populi Romani, but Horace may be simply returning to his first conception of ·Fortune as the goddess who rules the world.

29. Caesarem. It was in B.C. 26 that Augustus, then in Gaul, contemplated a campaign in Britain.

ultimos orbis Britannos. Cf. *Aeneid* VIII. 727 *extremi hominum Morini.*

30. recens examen. The expedition to Arabia, in which Iccius (I. 29) was to take part, seems to have been planned in B.C. 26, though it did not start till B.C. 24. The word *examen* (properly 'swarm' of bees) perhaps indicates the enthusiasm of the young volunteers.

32. Oceano rubro. The Indian Ocean.

34. fratrumque, sc. *occisorum,* referring to the civil wars.

35. nefasti for *nefandi,* 'of wickedness.' For the gen. cf. I. 3. 37.

37. metus deorum is piety. On the other hand *timor deorum* (*Sat.* II. 3. 295) is superstition.

38. nova. The epithet properly belongs to the swords, but is transferred by hypallage to the anvil. Cf. I. 3. 40.

39. diffingas, 'forge anew.' Properly *diffingere* is 'to change the form of,' as in III. 29. 47.

retunsum, 'blunted' in civil wars.

40. Massagetas. A tribe living near the Caspian Sea, to the N. E. of the Parthians. The neighbourhood of the Caucasus and the Caspian was of great interest to the Romans from B.C. 30 to 20, and is often mentioned in Horace. See especially II. 9.

Ode XXXVI.

Scheme. Let us give thanks to the gods who have brought back our Numida safe, to the delight of his old companions especially of Lamia. The day deserves a white mark. We will celebrate it with wine and dancing, and Damalis shall have a drinking-match with Bassus. We all love Damalis, but she will not leave the embrace of Numida.

It is not known who Numida was or whence he was returning.

NOTES.97

One scholiast calls him Pomponius N. another Plotius N. He may
have been in Spain at the Cantabrian war, from which Augustus
returned in B.C. 25.

Metre. Third Asclepiad.

1. **iuvat placare** is equivalent to *placemus.* Cf. III. 19. 8 *insanire
iuvat.*

2. **placare** is causal to *placere,* as *sedare* to *sedere.* It means 'to
make pleasing' and so 'to conciliate.' Cf. III. 23. 3.

debito. An offering was due *pro reditu felici.* So in II. 7. 17 there
is an *obligata daps* for the return of Pompeius.

4. **Hesperia,** obviously Spain.

6. **dividit** is appropriate to *multa oscula* in 5, but is employed in
l. 6 by zeugma.

7. **Lamiae.** See I. 26. 8 *n.*

8. **non alio rege,** abl. abs. 'under no other guide.' Lamia had
been *rex,* the ideal boy-friend, to Numida. Edd. however usually
interpret 'under the same schoolmaster,' as if N. and L. had been at
school together.

puertiae. Cf. *lamna* for *lamina* in II. 2. 2, *surpuerat* for *surri-
puerat* in IV. 13. 20, *erepsemus* for *erepsissemus* in *Sat.* I. 6.

9. **mutatae togae.** Children wore a purple-fringed toga, *praetexta,*
which they exchanged, about 15 years of age, for the *virilis,* which was
white.

10. **ne careat.** Kiessling suggests that this is a final clause: 'in
order that the day may not lack a white mark, let there be no stint of
wine or rest from the dance etc.'

Cressa nota, 'a chalk mark.' *Cressa* is properly the (Greek) fem.
of *Cres* 'a Cretan.' But the Latin for chalk is *creta,* and this name was
supposed to be derived from the island Crete, in much the same way as
fuller's earth was called Κιμωλία γῆ, from the island of Cimolus whence
it was procured. Lucky and unlucky days were apparently distinguished
by white and black marks in a calendar.

11. **promptae amphorae,** 'stint in bringing out the jar' or 'stint
of the jar when brought out.' For *promptae* cf. I. 9. 7.

12. **morem in Salium** (also in IV. 1. 28). *Salium* is the adj. for
Saliarem, Horace as usual avoiding the adjectival suffix: cf. *Dardanae
genti* in I. 15. 10.
The Salii were priests of Mars and were said to derive their name
from the dances which formed part of their ceremonies.

13. **multi Damalis meri.** Cf. *magni formica laboris* in *Sat.* I. 1.
33. Damalis is a great popular favourite: hence the repetition of her
name in 13, 17, 18.

14. **Bassum,** apparently a shy and sober person, but he is to drink
deep on this occasion. Martial (VI. 69) uses the name for a hard drinker.

amystide. ἄμυστις, in Greek, is a very large draught of wine, to

G. H. I.7

be drunk ἀμυστί 'without taking breath.' The *amystis* is more than once expressly attributed to the Thracians, who were great topers. (Cf. I. 18. 8 *n.*)

16. **apium**, cf. II. 7. 24.

breve, 'short-lived.' Cf. *breves flores rosae*, II. 3. 13.

17. **putris oculos**, 'languishing eyes.'

18. **nec**, 'but not.' Cf. II. 8. 18.

novo, i.e. Numida.

19. **adultero**, 'lover' (cf. I. 33. 9 *n.*), called *adulter* because he ousts the other lovers.

20. **lascivis**, 'wanton.'

ambitiosior, in its etymological meaning of 'clinging more closely.' Cf. *Epod.* 15. 5 *artius atque hedera...lentis adhaerens bracchiis*, and Shakespeare, *Midsummer-Night's Dream* IV. 1. 38, where Titania says to Bottom:

> 'Sleep thou and I will wind thee in my arms.
> So doth the woodbine the sweet honeysuckle
> Gently entwist; the female ivy so
> Enrings the barky fingers of the elm.
> O how I love thee! how I dote on thee!'

Ode XXXVII.

Scheme. Now we may drink and dance and set feasts before the gods, for Cleopatra is no more—Cleopatra who threatened our destruction. But her frenzied hate received a shock at Actium and turned into terror when Caesar pursued her, as a hawk pursues a dove. But she was a brave woman, fearing no shape of death, and too proud to figure as a captive in a Roman triumph.

This ode was evidently written in the autumn of B.C. 30, when Rome, after hearing of the capture of Alexandria and the death of Antony, received the further news of the suicide of Cleopatra. The ode is to some extent imitated from one by Alcaeus (see *Introd.* p. xxxix) on the death of Myrsilus, and appears to be one of Horace's earliest attempts in the Alcaic metre. (See ll. 5 and 14.)

2. **Saliaribus dapibus**, 'with feasts fit for the Salii.' The college of Salii were renowned for their choice dinners. Cf. also II. 14. 28 *mero pontificum potiore cenis*.

3. **ornare pulvinar deorum**. The reference is to the ceremony of a *lectisternium*, in which the images of the gods were brought out into the street, placed in pairs on sofas (*pulvinaria*) and served with a feast.

4. **tempus erat**, 'it is the right time' (though we did not think so), cf. I. 27. 19 *n.* A literal translation '*now* was the time etc.' gives quite the right sense, for the senate had decreed a *supplicatio*, or thanksgiving, on receiving the news of Antony's death and Horace means (as Kiessling points out) that *now*, after Cleopatra's death, is the better time for a thanksgiving. Orelli's version 'it was long since time' misses the point of the thrice-repeated *nunc*.

5. depromere, cf. I. 9. 7.

Caecubum, cf. I. 20. 9 *n.*
The absence of diaeresis (*Introd.* p. xxviii) in this line and in 14 recalls the practice of Alcaeus himself and is thought to indicate that Horace was still (B.C. 30) only a beginner in the composition of alcaics.

7. dementis. The epithet belongs to *regina* properly, cf. *iracunda fulmina* in I. 3. 40.

9. contaminato, 'with her foul crew of men hideous with disease.' *virorum* here means 'eunuchs' and, like *regina* in 7, is used spitefully.

10. impotens sperare like *praesens tollere* in I. 35. 2. *impotens* means 'unable to control herself,' like *incontinens* in I. 17. 26. Cf. Gr. ἀκρατής and ἐγκρατής.

13. vix una sospes navis, i.e. the fact that barely a single ship was rescued, cf. I. 13. 19 where *divolsus amor* means 'the rupture of love' and II. 4. 10 where *ademptus Hector* means 'the death of Hector.' Cf. also III. 4. 26.
Horace here does some little violence to history, for it was Antony's fleet that was burnt at Actium, while Cleopatra's fled.

14. On the scansion cf. l. 5 *n.*

lymphatam, 'delirious.'

Mareotico, a sweet wine produced on the shores of lake Mareotis, close to Alexandria.

15. veros timores, opposed to the false terrors of delirium tremens.

17. adurgens, 'pressing her hard' in pursuit. This is another liberty taken with history, for Octavian did not follow Cleopatra to Alexandria till B.C. 30, a year after Actium.

20. Haemoniae, 'Thessaly,' called *nivalis* 'snow-clad,' because hares were hunted in winter, cf. *Sat.* I. 2. 105 *leporem venator ut alta In nive sectetur.*

daret ut catenis. Octavian expressly wished to take Cleopatra alive, that she might be shown in his triumph.

21. fatale monstrum, 'a deadly horror,' like the Sphinx or the Chimaera.

quae. The grammatical antecedent is *monstrum*, meaning Cleopatra. The construction is *ad sensum*. So Cicero, speaking of Clodius (*Fam.* I. 9. 15), calls him *illa furia...qui.*

21. generosius, in a manner more worthy of her noble blood.

23. expavit ensem. Plutarch, in his life of Antonius (c. 79), says that Cleopatra tried to stab herself when she was captured by Proculeius. He also says (c. 69) that she had previously tried to transport her fleet over the isthmus of Suez with intent to escape by the Red Sea.

nec latentis...oras. The text means 'nor did she with her swift fleet procure in exchange (for Egypt) a home in some hidden land.' The meaning here assigned to *reparavit* is founded on that assigned to *reparata* in I. 31. 12, but (see note there) the meaning of that passage is not quite certain and *classe reparavit* ought to mean 'procured in exchange for her fleet.' Hence the numerous conjectures mentioned in the critical note.

25—32. Here follow at least three parallel adjectival clauses, beginning *ausa—ferocior—invidens.* (Most editors even make four, regarding *fortis et tractare* etc. as a separate clause.) This is regarded as a sign of Horace's imperfect command of the metre.

25. iacentem, 'grief-stricken.' *regiam* is 'her court.' Cleopatra was taken to her palace after her capture by Proculeius.

26. fortis is more conveniently taken with *vultu sereno* in which case the *et...et* can mean 'both...and.' But most edd. construct *fortis* with *tractare* (cf. *Introd.* p. xxiii) and translate *et* 'even' in both lines.

asperas, 'angry.'

28. combiberet. It is a well-known tale that Cleopatra caused herself to be bitten by an asp.

29. deliberata...ferocior, 'more proud than ever when she had resolved to die.' *delib. morte* is abl. abs.

30. Liburnis, dat. after *invidens*: 'begrudging the fierce Liburnians.' Some edd. however regard *Liburnis* as abl. of *Liburnae* i.e. 'Liburnian ships' (cf. *Epod.* 1. 1), notwithstanding the epithet *saevis*.

31. privata, 'dethroned,' 'unqueened.'

deduci is direct obj. to *invidens*: 'begrudging that she should be led.'

32. non humilis, 'haughty,' cf. 1. 18. 9 *non levis.*

triumpho is usually taken as abl.: 'that she should be dragged unqueened in the insolent triumph.' Kiessling, however, regards it as dat. after *deduci*, 'be dragged *to* the triumph,' like *compulerit gregi* in I. 24. 18.

Ode XXXVIII.

1. Persicos apparatus, 'Persian kickshaws.' Apparently scents and ointments are meant: cf. III. 1. 44 *Achaemenium costum.* Both Page and Kiessling note that the *ad-* of *apparatus* and *allabores* suggests the idea of excess.

puer is addressed to the slave who waits at table.

2. philyra, 'bast.' *philyra* is properly the Greek name of the lime-tree, called in Latin *tilia.* The inner bark of this tree was used for tying garlands, or sometimes the flowers were stitched on it (hence *sutiles coronae*).

3. mitte = *omitte*, cf. III. 8. 17.

quo locorum = *quo loco* only.

5. myrto, the plant sacred to Venus.

allabores, a word peculiar to Horace (used again in *Epod.* 8. 20). It is dependent on *curo*: cf. *volo facias* etc. 'I am particular that you do not trouble to add.'

6. sedulus with *allabores.*

7. sub arta vite. The vine is trained over a trellis, so that the leaves lie close together and make an arbour.

CONSPECTUS METRORUM.

I. Alcmanium :

   – ⏗ – ⏗ –, ⏗ – ⏗ – ∪ ∪ – ⏝   hexam. dactyl.

   – ⏗ – ⏗ – ∪ ∪ – ⏝   tetramet. dact. catalect.

   c. I 7. 28. epod. 12.

II. Archilochīum quartum :

   – ⏗ – ⏗ – ⏗ – ∪ ∪, – ∪ – ∪ – ∪   versus Archilo-
                                        chīus maior.

   ⏝ – ∪ – ⏝, – ∪ – ∪ – ⏝   trimet. iamb. catal.

   c. I 4.

III. Asclepiadēum primum :

   – – – ∪ ∪ –, – ∪ ∪ – ∪ ⌣   versus Asclepiadēus
   c. I 1. III 30. IV 8.   minor.

IV. Asclepiadēum secundum sive maius :

   – – – ∪ ∪ –, – ∪ ∪ –, – ∪ ∪ – ∪ ⌣   versus Asclepi-
   c. I 11. 18. IV 10.   adēus maior.

V. Asclepiadēum tertium :

   – – – ∪ ∪ – ∪ ⌣   versus Glyconēus.

   – – – ∪ ∪ –, – ∪ ∪ – ∪ ⌣   v. Asclepiadēus minor.

   c. I 3. 13. 19. 36. III 9. 15. 19. 24. 25. 28. IV 1. 3.

VI.   Sapphicum maius:

−∪∪−∪−⏕   versus Aristophanīus.

−∪−−−, ∪∪−, −∪∪−∪−⏔ versus Sapphicus
c. I 8.   maior.

VII.   Asclepiadēum quartum :

−−−∪∪−, −∪∪−∪⏔   v. Asclepiadēus minor.

−−−∪∪−, −∪∪−∪⏔   „

−−−∪∪−, −∪∪−∪⏔   „

−−−∪∪−∪⏔   v. Glyconēus.

c. I 6. 15. 24. 33. II 12. III 10. 16. IV 5. 12.

VIII.   Asclepiadēum quintum :

−−−∪∪−, −∪∪−∪⏔   v. Asclepiadēus minor.

−−−∪∪−, −∪∪−∪⏔   „   „

−−−∪∪−⏕   v. Pherecratēus secun-
                    dus acatal.

−−−∪∪−∪⏔   v. Glyconēus.

c. I 5. 14. 21. 23. III 7. 13. IV 13.

IX.   Sapphicum minus :

−∪−−−, ∪∪−∪−⏕   versus Sapphicus minor
                    hendecasyllabus.

−∪−−−, ∪∪−∪−⏕   „   „

−∪−−−, ∪∪−∪−⏕   „   „

−∪∪−⏕   v. Adonius.

c. I 2. 10. 12. 20. 22. 25. 30. 32. 38. II 2. 4. 6. 8.
10. 16. III 8. 11. 14. 18. 20. 22. 27. IV. 2. 6.
11. carm. saec.

X. Alcaicum metrum :

⏑ − ⏑ − −, − ⏑ ⏑ − ⏑ ⏒   **v.** Alcaicus hendeca-
                                   syllabus.

⏑ − ⏑ − −, − ⏑ ⏑ − ⏑ ⏒   „   „
⏑ − ⏑ − − − ⏑ − ⏑   **v.** Alcaicus enneasyl-
                                   labus.

     − ⏑ ⏑ − ⏑ ⏑ − ⏑ − ⏑   **v.** Alcaicus decasyl-
                                   labus.

c. I 9. 16. 17. 26. 27. 29. **31.** 34. 35. 37. II **1.** 3.
5. 7. 9. **11.** **13.** 14. 15. **17.** 19. 20. III 1—6. 17.
21. **23.** 26. 29. IV 4. 9. **14.** **15.**

For EU product safety concerns, contact us at Calle de José Abascal, 56–1°,
28003 Madrid, Spain or eugpsr@cambridge.org.